Insight through Learning, Reflecting, and Meditating:

The Fourfold Application of Mindfulness

Shamar Rinpoche

Series

Bird of Paradise Press

ABOUT BIRD OF PARADISE PRESS

Bird of Paradise Press is a non-profit book publisher based in the United States. The press specializes in Buddhist meditation and philosophy, as well as other topics from Buddhist perspectives including history, ethics, and governance. Its books are distributed worldwide and available in multiple languages. The bird mentioned in the company's name is said to be from a special place where beings can meet with favorable conditions to progress on their path to awakening.

Also by Shamar Rinpoche

BRINGING MIND TRAINING TO LIFE
An Exploration of the 5th Shamarpa's Concise Lojong Manual

THE PATH TO AWAKENING
How Buddhism's Seven Points of Mind Training Can Lead You to a Life of Enlightenment and Happiness

BOUNDLESS AWAKENING
The Heart of Buddhist Meditation

BOUNDLESS WISDOM
A Mahāmudrā Practice Manual

A GOLDEN SWAN IN TURBULENT WATERS
The Life and Times of the Tenth Karmapa Choying Dorje

THE KING OF PRAYERS
A Commentary on the Noble King of Prayers of Excellent Conduct

CREATING A TRANSPARENT DEMOCRACY
A New Model

BUDDHA NATURE
Our Potential for Wisdom, Compassion, and Happiness

A PATH OF PRACTICE
The Bodhi Path Program

Shamar Rinpoche

Insight through Learning, Reflecting, and Meditating:

The Fourfold Application of Mindfulness

Explanations Based on
"*The Commentary on the Discourse of Defining the Topics*"
(Arthaviniścayasūtraṭīka)

Translated, edited, and introduced
by Martina Draszczyk

RABSEL
PUBLICATIONS

Insight through Learning, Reflecting, and Meditating:
The Fourfold Application of Mindfulness

Explanations Based on "*The Commentary on the Discourse of Defining the Topics*" (*Arthaviniścayasūtraṭīka*) given in Dhagpo Kagyu Ling (2006)

Translated, edited and introduced by Martina Draszczyk

This project was supported by the DRAC and Normandy Region under the FADEL Normandie, France.

PRÉFET DE LA RÉGION NORMANDIE
Liberté Égalité Fraternité

RÉGION NORMANDIE

RABSEL PUBLICATIONS
16, rue de Babylone
76430 La Remuée, France
www.rabsel.com
contact@rabsel.com

ISBN 978-2-36017-067-8

Contents

A Note on Foreign Terms

Because Sanskrit and Tibetan terms appear frequently throughout this book, they are given in *italics* only at their first occurance. Where I considered it preferable for the sake of simplicity to retain either Tibetan or Sanskrit terms, I have generally opted for the Sanskrit terms (with diacritics). Unlike the Sanskrit transliteration, the exact transliteration of the Tibetan is challenging to read for all those who are not familiar with the Wylie transliteration system. For this reason, I have employed a simple phonetic rendering of the Tibetan words and names while the notes give the precise transliteration.

Preface
by Jigme Rinpoche

Mipham Chökyi Lodrö, the 14th Shamar Rinpoché, passed into parinirvana in 2014. Ten years have gone by already since he left this world, yet he is very much present in the Dharma centres implementing the curriculum of learning and meditative practice that he systematised. Following in the footsteps of Rangjung Rikpé Dorjé, the 16th Gyalwa Karmapa, Shamar Rinpoché's concern was to make the Dharma available in the most genuine way.

From 1988 to 2014, students at Dhagpo Kagyu Ling were extremely fortunate and blessed to receive him every single year, and sometimes more than once a year. Shamar Rinpoché took care to offer the nectar of the Buddha's words and methods so that practitioners could journey on the path toward liberation.

I thus truly rejoice that Martina Draszczyk and Rabsel Éditions are pursuing their contribution to Shamar Rinpoché's curriculum by rendering accessible, in the present book, the teaching he gave at Dhagpo Kagyu Ling in 2006 on the Fourfold Application of Mindfulness entitled *Insight through Learning, Reflecting, and Meditating.*

This teaching is the perfect combination of a theoretical approach joined to a meditative practice so as to acquire a true discernment, an insight, of what our current state and environment is: impermanence, suffering, emptiness and inexistence of true identity. These four characteristics of the truth of suffering are experienced through the Buddhist process of learning, reflecting and meditating.

I would like to request every student to please learn, to please reflect, and to please meditate so as to recognize the state of samsara; abandon its causes; actualize its cessation; and rely on the path leading to freedom from suffering.

May sentient beings gain insight into what actually creates unhappiness and what truly leads to happiness.

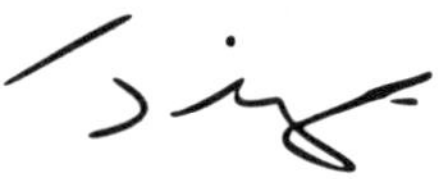

Lama Jigmé Rinpoché

Dhagpo Kagyu Ling
February 29, 2024

Introduction
by the Translator

I am delighted to publish these explanations on the fourfold application of mindfulness. Kunzig Shamar Rinpoche gave these teachings in a series of lectures at Dhagpo Kagyu Ling (France) in the summer of 2006. He revisited this topic during a second set of lectures at Dhagpo Kagyu Ling; this was shortly before his passing in 2014. These instructions from 2014, which were notably practical, are published in *The Buddha's Gift to the World* (2024, chapter 4).[1]

In the explanations provided here from the year 2006, Shamar Rinpoche delved into the theoretical background. He drew upon an excerpt from the sūtra *The Dharma Discourse on Defining the Topics* (*Artha-viniścaya Dharmaparyāya*) and used a commentary to

1 Draszczyk, Martina. 2024. *The Buddha's Gift to the World. A Practitioner's Guide to the Roots of Mindfulness. An Exploration across Indian and Tibetan Traditions.* Boulder: Shambhala Publications.

go into the details, *The Commentary on the Discourse of Defining the Topics* (*Arthaviniścayasūtraṭīka*). He deliberately adopted this classical approach, which is why the instructions may at times appear somewhat theoretical. Let us therefore place these teachings within the context of meditation practice; which is what I would like to briefly address at this point.

In the fourfold application of mindfulness, the meditation practices of calm abiding (*śamatha; shiné*) and deep insight (*vipaśyanā; lhagthong*)[2] converge; ideally, they mutually reinforce each other.

We train in calm abiding by directing our attention with the support of a specific object or topic (such as the breath or loving kindness) toward awareness in the present moment, and by sustaining this inner calm—mindfully and clearly knowing. The more peaceful and stable the mind becomes through this training, the more joyful, relaxed, and clear it will be. Shamar Rinpoche has provided precise instructions on this, which can be found, for example, in *A Way of Practice: The Bodhi Path Curriculum* or in his *Boundless Wisdom: A Handbook for Mahāmudrā Practice*.

We train in deep insight by exploring and discerning the nature of experiences. Cultivating the understanding gained thereby will bring about a transformation in our habitual clinging to conditioned notions and projections; it will gradually dissolve our delusions. Detailed instructions from Shamar Rinpoche on deep insight can be found in *Boundless*

---

2 "Calm abiding." Sanskrit: *śamatha*; Tibetan phonetics: *shiné*; Tibetan transliteration: *zhi gnas*. "Deep insight." Sanskrit: vipaśyanā; Tibetan phonetics: *lhagthong*; Tibetan transliteration: *lhag mthong*).

Wisdom and in chapter four of *The Buddha's Gift to the World.*

In the course of the fourfold application of mindfulness, the process of generating insight (*prajñā*; *sherab*)[3] unfolds gradually: the initial step involves learning about it. Then we gain more clarity through reflection. Ultimately, insight can become a direct and more constant experience if we invest enough time to familiarize ourselves with this view in meditation. These steps of learning, reflecting, and meditating may initially appear linear—as if one were to progressively learn the steps of a specific dance. Yet, they become more intuitive with practice, akin to dancers who are familiar with their steps and instinctively know the next move.

As mentioned above, the fourfold application of mindfulness is about practicing deep insight, building on the foundation of calm abiding. The practice involves examining (1) the body, (2) feelings, (3) the mind, and (4) mental phenomena, from various vantage points and abiding in the insights gained thereby. In our everyday consciousness, that is to say, in a non-reflective, conditioned state, we typically experience the body, feelings, the mind, and mental phenomena very subjectively. They are the frame of reference for our life and function as the breeding ground for our identity as we perceive it. Naturally, our experience of these four is based on our socialization, the views and opinions we acquired over time, life experiences, and habits. Usually, we experience our body as a somehow constant and unified center

3 "Insight." Sanskrit: *prajñā*; Tibetan phonetics: *sherab*; Tibetan transliteration: *shes rab.*

of our sense of self and our place in the world. We believe that our feelings can and will truly make us happy and invest a lot in pursuing this. We consider our current state of mind as our true identity, and we attribute a certain independent, self-existing objective reality to everything we go through and experience, that is, to mental phenomena. In all four areas, that is, the body, feelings, mind, and mental phenomena, we deceive ourselves significantly. Furthermore, the way we experience both body and mind is frequently accompanied by tension, pain, and dissatisfaction. This is partly because what we hope for in our lives does not materialize or only does so to a limited extent. Moreover, our conditioned experience is continuously enhanced by a subliminal and often unconscious clinging to our perceptions. The extent of this clinging determines the level of constriction or expansiveness we experience in our lives. As we gradually release this clinging, we pave the way for freedom to blossom in our lives.

The spiritual practice of applying mindfulness is akin to a spotlight directed at the body, feelings, the mind, and mental phenomena. Illuminated by the warm light of attention, we clearly recognize their manifestation in our lives and their true nature. In this caring ambience of meditation, we gradually recognize our delusions as delusions—in the same way that we can see through the illusions presented by a magician. We experience the changing and ultimately substanceless nature of everything, without clinging or rejecting, aware, and awake. The key to this meditation practice is observing the present experience without attempting to change it. The inner power of calm abiding and deep insight provides the stability and clarity needed to let go of our automated clinging to the "reality" we are used to. Consequently, and without struggle, the habit of clinging to concepts of "I," "mine," "self," and "other" fades away. This training, that we could call receptive non-intervention, allows us to become more aware of our inner processes, subtle motives, and involuntary reactions. The more we familiarize ourselves with this experience of observing, allowing, letting be, and letting go in the focused "laboratory" of formal meditation, the more our perception of the outer world and our self-perception changes from within. Naturally this leads to a transformation of our emotional and mental world. We experience more peace and equanimity and learn to deal with life in beneficial ways. This, according to the Buddha, is a direct path to end the suffering.

The source for these teachings

Shamar Rinpoche's explanations are based on the following excerpt from *The Dharma Discourse of Defining the Topics* (*Arthaviniścaya Dharmaparyāya*)[4];

---

4 *The Dharma Discourse of Defining the Topics* (*The Arthaviniścaya Dharmaparyāya*) is extant in Sanskrit, Tibetan, and Chinese. The title of the Tibetan version is *Don rnam par nges pa zhes bya ba'i chos kyi rnam grangs*. It is contained in the Tibetan Kangyur (vol. 72, Derge D 317, 170b4-188a7 and Lhasa H 321, 262b6-289a1). It was translated twice into Chinese; the first time by Faxian (法賢; 10th c., Taishō 762 決定義經), a second time by Jin Zong Chi (金總持; 11th c., Taishō 763 法乘義決定經). It was rendered into English by N.H. Samtani and published in *Gathering the Meanings. Essential Teachings of the Buddha. The Arthaviniścaya Sūtra with its Commentary Nibandhana*, 3-42. Berkeley, CA: Dharma Publications 2002; reprinted, Delhi: Motilal Banarsidass 2005. Samtani edited and translated the Sanskrit version already in 1971: *The Arthaviniścaya-sūtra and its Commentary (Nibandhana by Bhikṣu Vīryaśridatta)*. Patna: J. P. Jayaswal Research Institute, 1971.

this text is considered a discourse or sūtra taught by Buddha Śākyamuni:

> Oh monks, what in this context, is the fourfold application of mindfulness?
>
> Monks, here practitioners—who are diligent, clearly knowing and mindful, free from any desires and discontent[5] in regard to the world—constantly contemplate the body with regard to the inner body.
>
> Diligent, clearly knowing and mindful, free from any desires and discontent in regard to the world, they constantly contemplate phenomena: the inner body, the outer body, and both the inner and outer body; the inner feelings, the outer feelings, and both the inner and outer feelings; the inner mind, the outer mind, and both the inner and outer mind as well as the inner mental phenomena [*dharmas*], the outer mental phenomena, and both

5 We can see this also as a preparation for the practice of mindfulness prior to which practitioners deliberately decide to let go from being entangled in worldly matters. "Free from any desires" thus refers to a state of mind in which attachments are relinquished, at least for the time period of meditation. "Free from discontent" refers to a state of mind free from aversion and anger, so that the mind remains calm and free from discontentment.

the inner and outer mental phenomena.[6]

The passage above outlines the fourfold application of mindfulness in just a few words, forming the beginning of the so-called "Thirty-seven Factors Conducive to Awakening".[7]

6 The translation was done based on the Tibetan edition of the *Artha-viniścaya Sūtra* in Kangyur H 321, vol. 72, *la* 262b-289a. Tibetan: *Don rnam par nges pa zhes bya ba'i chos kyi rnam grangs*, quote: 274b4-275a1. The phrasing is slightly different from the one found in *Gathering the Meanings. Essential Teachings of the Buddha. The Arthaviniścaya Sūtra with its Commentary Nibandhana* which contains a translation from the original Sanskrit.

7 The Thirty-Seven Factors Conducive to Awakening are grouped under seven headings. *Group one*, the fourfold application of mindfulness: The application of mindfulness with regard to the body; the application of mindfulness with regard to feelings; the application of mindfulness with regard to the mind; and the application of mindfulness with regard to mental phenomena/dharmas/dhammas. *Group two*, the four ways of right endeavor: Not allowing what is unwholesome to arise again; overcoming the unwholesome that has already arisen; allowing what is wholesome to arise; and cultivating and enhancing the wholesome that has already arisen. *Group three*, the four grounds for special capabilities: intention; joyful effort; mental directionality; and investigation. *Group four*, the five faculties: confidence; joyful effort; mindfulness; meditative absorption; and insight. *Group five*, the five powers: confidence; joyful effort; mindfulness; meditative absorption; and insight. *Group six*, the seven factors of awakening: mindfulness; discernment of phenomena; joyful effort; joy; pliancy; meditative absorption; and equanimity. *Group seven*, the noble eightfold path: right/wise view; right/wise intention; right/wise speech; right/wise action; right/wise livelihood; right/wise joyful effort; right/wise mindfulness; and right/wise meditative absorption.

The sūtra ends as follows:

> Monks, the Dharma that I teach you is about pure conduct. It is beneficial in the beginning, beneficial in the middle, and beneficial in the end. The meaning is outstanding. The word choice is excellent. It is not confused. It is perfect, it is pure, clear, and purifying. This, *The Dharma Discourse on Defining the Topics* (*Arthaviniścaya Dharmaparyāya*), is the Dharma that I have presented to you in its entirety. Monks, sitting in stable concentration, you should definitely practice according to these explanations, be it in hermitages, under trees, in empty huts, in the mountains, in mountain caves, in straw huts, unprotected in the open, in cemeteries or in forest clearings. Do not live imprudently! Otherwise, you will surely regret it later! This is my instruction for you![8]

In his explanations of the fourfold application of mindfulness, Shamar Rinpoche followed, as mentioned above, the *Commentary on the Discourse of De-*

8 *Arthaviniścaya Sūtra,* Tibetan: *Don rnam par nges pa zhes bya ba'i chos kyi rnam grangs*, Lhasa H 321, 288a7-288b7.

fining the Topics (*Arthaviniścayasūtraṭīka*).[9] This commentary is a classical Abhidharma treatise, which so far is only available in the Tibetan language. It is contained in the Tengyur, the Tibetan collection of recognized Buddhist treatises or *śāstras*. Most of the treatises in the Tengyur stem from India, were originally written in Sanskrit and later translated into Tibetan—hence the name of this collection as "Tengyur," meaning "translated treatises." However, there are also some śāstras in the Tengyur that were written directly in Tibetan and therefore are not translations from Sanskrit. Since neither author nor translator are disclosed in *The Commentary on the Dharma Discourse of Determining the Topics*, it cannot be determined with certainty whether it is actually a translation, though the probability is high.

In Tibetan, *The Commentary on the Dharma Discourse of Determining the Topics* is the only currently existing commentary on *The Dharma Discourse of Determining the Topics*. However, there is another similar but shorter commentary preserved in Sanskrit. The title of this Sanskrit work is *Gathering the*

9 *The Commentary on Defining the Topics* (*Arthaviniścayasūtraṭīka*). Tibetan: *Don rnam par gdon mi za ba'i 'grel pa*. This commentary is contained in the Tibetan Tengyurs, for example in Derge (D 4365) *sna tshogs, nyo* 1b1-192a7, vol. 208, Peking (Q 5852) *ngo mtshar bstan bcos, jo* 1a1-221a5 (vol. 145), and Narthang (N 4618) *ngo mtshar bstan bcos, jo* 1b1-215a7. Neither the author nor the translator are known. The text is also not contained in the early Tibetan catalogues of Buddhist scriptures, the *Lhan kar ma* and the 'Phang thang ma. *Lhan kar ma* (730B) lists a text that would be interesting in the context of the application of mindfulness, the *Dran pa nye bar gzhag pa chen po* (**Mahāsmṛtyupasthāna*). Unfortunately, this text is lost and there exists no additional information about it. I thank Prof. Helmut Tauscher for this information.

Meaning Regarding the Discourse of Defining the Topics (*Arthaviniścaya Sūtra Nibandhana*).[10] The author is bhikṣu Vīryaśridatta, who lived in the eighth century and taught in the great Buddhist monastic university of Nālandā. There seems to be no Tibetan translation of this commentary.

The Dharma Discourse of Determining the Topics deals with twenty-seven classical Abhidharma topics, which form the basis for the practice of Buddhist meditation. The topics are: (1) the five aggregates or *skandhas*,[11] (2) the five skandhas affected by clinging, (3) the eighteen elements of perception, (4) the twelve sense fields, (5) the twelvefold dependent arising, (6) the four noble truths, (7) the twenty-two faculties, (8) the four levels of meditative absorption, (9) the four levels of formlessness, (10) the four sublime states, (11) the four stages of meditation, (12) the four ways of attaining concentration, (13) the fourfold application of mindfulness, (14) the four types of right endeavor, (15) the four grounds for special capabilities, (16) the five faculties, (17) the five powers, (18) the seven factors of awakening, (19) the noble eightfold path, (20) the sixteenfold mindfulness with the breath, (21) the four aspects of stream entry, (22) the powers of a *tathāgata*, (23) the fourfold fearlessness of a Tathāgata, (24) the four

---

10 This Sanskrit commentary was translated into English by N. H. Samtani and published in 2002 with the title *Gathering the Meanings. Essential Teachings of the Buddha. The Arthaviniścaya Sūtra with its Commentary Nibandhana*. For details, see note 4.

11 According to the *Arthaviniścaya Sūtra Nibandhana* "skandha" pertains to the pure skandhas of yogis who accomplished states of realization. See *Gathering the Meanings. Essential Teachings of the Buddha. The Arthaviniścaya Sūtra with its Commentary Nibandhana,* 56-57.

types of the particular awareness of a Tathāgata, (25) the eighteen qualities that are unique to a Buddha, (26) the thirty-two defining characteristics of a great being, a Tathāgata, and (27) the eighty characteristics of a Buddha.

Of the above Dharma topics, Shamar Rinpoche chose one of them: the fourfold application of mindfulness. As stated above, this forms the start for a series of topics that extend from points thirteen to nineteen, and which are all added together in the Thirty-seven Factors Conducive to Awakening. At the end of his explanations, Shamar Rinpoche expressed his hope that the listeners will in future also study the further aspects of these thirty-seven factors.

The focus of the explanations presented here

In his explanations, Shamar Rinpoche focused on developing insight through listening/learning, reflecting, and meditating on the so called "specific and general characteristics"[12] of the body, feelings, mind, and mental phenomena. The distinction between specific characteristics and generalizing or general characteristics is an important part of Buddhist epistemology. However, in the context of the fourfold application of mindfulness, these terms are also used in a slightly different way. Shamar Rinpoche focused in his explanation on these different perspectives.

12 Specific characteristic (Sanskrit: *svalakṣana*; Tibetan phonetics: *rang tsen; Tibetan transliteration: rang mtshan*). Generalizing/general characteristic (Sanskrit: *sāmānya lakṣaṇa*; Tibetan phonetics: *chi tsen*; Tibetan transliteration: *spyl mtshan*).

The specific characteristic

In Buddhist epistemology, the term "specific characteristic" refers to the "thing in itself," independent of our labeling and our conceptual notions of it. The body's specific characteristic is that it consists of countless finest particles or cells which comprise the "ingredients" of the elements (solidity, fluidity, temperature, movement) and which are subject to constant change and renewal. It is therefore subtle impermanence. In this constant flow of change, the cells of the body fulfill their respective functions while they have no true or autonomous nature of their own. This principle applies equally to the other reference points, to feelings, mind, and mental phenomena.

The generalizing characteristic

In contrast to the specific characteristic, the terms "body," "feelings," "mind," and "mental phenomena" are simply labels or attributions. We have learned to associate these generalizing terms or notions with incessantly changing phenomena. In Buddhist epistemology this is called "generalizing characteristic" and differentiated to the term "specific characteristic." In short, the term "generalizing characteristic" refers to the ability of abstraction by means of which our consciousness—based on multisensory and constantly changing inputs—generates coherent mental images and links them with meanings. Through this skill, we constantly construct how we perceive our world and relate phenomena to each other.

These processes take place through conceptualizations and generalizations, whereby we assign terms, names, categories, evaluations, and the like to what we experience externally and/or internally. Here is a case in point: As explained above, even though our own appearance is subject to a dynamic process of constantly changing cells, we put the label "body" on it and identify ourselves with it as "my body."

It is important to take into consideration that this distinction between "specific" and "generalizing" characteristics does initially not constitute a judgement as such; it just constitutes different aspects of experiencing and perceiving something. However, problems, conflicts, and suffering arise when we have not learned to distinguish between the specific and generalizing characteristics or, in other words, when we mistake our subjective notions for *the* objective reality. For this reason, it is very helpful to learn how to distinguish between these two.

However, in connection with the fourfold application of mindfulness, the term "general characteristic" has a broader meaning. Based on the specific characteristic, "general characteristic" in this instance denotes what is common to all phenomena, that is, bodies, feelings, the mind, and mental phenomena. They all have the general characteristics of impermanence, emptiness, the absence of a true identity, and suffering as a feature of all experiences that involve self-attachment or clinging.

The fourfold application of mindfulness and the two characteristics

The starting point in the practice of the fourfold application of mindfulness is the contemplation on the "specific characteristic": as mentioned above, the specific characteristic of physical bodies is that they consist of the various elements; they are accumulations of countless particles or cells in constant change. In fact, this applies to every kind of body, that is to say one's own body or the body of others, or even form, sound, smell, taste, and tangible things. The specific characteristic of feelings is experiencing or sensing something, and we are constantly feeling something, whether it is pleasant, unpleasant or neither pleasant nor unpleasant. The specific characteristic of the mind is knowing, recognizing or perceiving something; it is about our dynamic states of mind, our thoughts, emotions, memories, and associations, be they positive or negative. The specific characteristic of mental phenomena is that they can be known. All in all, these specific characteristics form something like our social reality; that is, within the framework of our conventions, we experience them as real and we identify ourselves with them. When contemplating the "specific characteristic," the focus therefore is initially on understanding the body, feelings, the mind, and mental phenomena as they are, with their specific features or characteristics.

On this basis we devote ourselves to the contemplation of the so-called "general characteristics." We do so in order to deepen our understanding of how our delusion operates in relation to body, feelings, the mind, and mental phenomena: these four have in common that they are impermanent; more precisely, they change from moment to moment. They are interdependent, and are therefore without a constant, autonomous, self-existing nature of their own; in this sense, they are selfless or essenceless. Moreover, all experiences that are clouded by self-clinging will inevitably lead to suffering.

At a time when we are not yet experienced in our practice, we will, in fact, partly experience these general characteristics—impermanence, emptiness, the absence of a true identity, and suffering as a characteristic of all experiences accompanied by self-clinging—as generalizing characteristics. That is, we develop a mental image of subtle impermanence, of emptiness, and of the absence of a true identity. Our mental skills of forming abstractions, conceptualizing, and knowing what the generalizing characteristics consists of, enables us to develop an understanding of these common features of phenomena. Eventually, and by virtue of deep meditation, we can finally comprehend subtle impermanence, emptiness and the absence of a true identity, and the various aspects of suffering directly and without generalization or abstraction. Developing this profound and direct insight is the purpose of the practice.

The generalizing/general characteristics

To make the different uses of the term "generalizing/general characteristics" in Shamar Rinpoche's explanations easily recognizable, I translated it partly as "generalizing characteristic" and partly as "general characteristic."

"Generalizing" is used when it is about conceptualizing, generalizing, and attributing. "General" is used to describe what is common to all external and internal conditions: impermanence, emptiness and the absence of a true identity, and suffering as a characteristic of all experiences accompanied by self-clinging.

*****

As already mentioned, Shamar Rinpoche taught the topic of the fourfold application of mindfulness in Dhagpo Kagyu Ling twice. In 2014 he concentrated his explanations on meditation as such, linking it also to the Mahāmudrā instructions,[13] whereas in 2006, he focused on the necessary framework for it. As an inspiration for one's own practice, it is therefore highly recommended to study both sets of instructions.

These lectures took place in the summer of 2006. Shamar Rinpoche taught almost invariably in Tibetan; the interpreter into French was Trinley Tulku Rinpoche. My translation from Tibetan into English presented here was based on the audio recording of the teachings. In my translation I tried to remain faithful to Shamar Rinpoche's presentation in Tibetan. I did not emend a number of repetitions, since they occur naturally in oral teachings. I left out some brief passages that were not directly connected with the topic. These omissions are marked with omission signs (...). I also rearranged some passages to facilitate the orientation in the written version. Therefore, the order in the text does not always correspond to the oral lecture. Additionally, I inserted a number of

13 See note 1.

headings to make the structure more easily recognizable. These headings are based on the Tibetan commentary that Shamar Rinpoche relied on.

At this point, I would like to express my gratitude first and foremost to Kunzig Shamar Rinpoche (1952–2014) who generously shared these teachings with us. Secondly I wish to thank Ven. Jigme Rinpoche, the spiritual director of Dhagpo Kagyu Ling, for permission and encouragement to translate and publish these teachings. I also want to express my appreciation to everyone involved in the editorial process, in particular to Timothy Riese, Karin Höhl, and Rachel Parrish for correcting my English. Last but not least, I would like to thank Rabsel Éditions for publishing books of this nature. Inevitably in an undertaking of this kind, mistakes and misunderstandings may have slipped in. It goes without saying that all such errors are entirely mine, and I would welcome any suggestions and corrections, which can hopefully be included in a subsequent revised edition.

May what is wholesome and virtuous increase.

Insight through Learning, Reflecting, and Meditating: The Fourfold Application of Mindfulness Explanations Based on *The Commentary on Defining the Topics*

Introduction

We are very fortunate to have come together here to study the Dharma. About two thousand five hundred years ago,[14] Buddha Śākyamuni set in motion the so-called Wheel of Dharma by teaching the Four Noble Truths in our world. The Buddha's teachings have not degenerated during this long period but have continued to unfold and expand. That is something truly extraordinary. More than thirty years ago, the Dharma also found its way to the West. We find ourselves in an exceptionally fortunate situation. Despite the ongoing devastating conflicts in various parts of the world, we are still in a very fortunate position

14 Shamar Rinpoche added that depending on the way you count it, also three thousand years have passed.

compared to historical periods like the dark Middle Ages. Presently, many people have the opportunity to lead fulfilling lives (...). Furthermore, the average life expectancy has significantly increased; many enjoy good health and reach the age of eighty or even ninety—unlike in the past when people typically lived to be sixty to seventy years old. Additionally, numerous ailments that were once incurable can now be cured because effective medication is widely available. (...) A comparison with beings in heavenly realms also highlights the unique nature of our human existence. Heavenly beings experience extraordinary happiness and enjoyments. However, lacking the presence of the Buddha Dharma in those realms, they squander their long pleasant lives, distracted by the luxuries available in these realms. When their lifespan eventually comes to an end, other karmic tendencies from previous lives mature. Despite their blissful existence, their minds remain tainted by self-clinging and mental defilements; no samsaric being is entirely free from them. Consequently, depending on which tendencies of defilements and karma manifest during death, these will mature and may lead to a rebirth in painful states of existence.

In our present existence, we have a precious human life. The Buddha's teachings are widely available, spanning across the globe, whether in the East or the West. Numerous individuals place their trust in the authenticity of the Dharma and aspire to follow its path. While not everyone possesses all the necessary conditions for such a pursuit, many have confidence in the Dharma. In this regard, our world provides an environment where a human life, equipped with the eighteen freedoms and opportunities[15] essential for Dharma practice, is exceptionally valuable. With these favorable conditions, our world takes on the semblance of a pure Buddha realm. Nevertheless, in such an era of well-being, if you merely indulge in the pleasures of life without engaging in Dharma practice and contemplation of impermanence, you risk wasting this precious life. Having come into contact with the Dharma, it is therefore crucial to reflect upon and internalize the teachings. Individuals unfamiliar with the Dharma lack an understanding of this necessity and consequently find no access to this spiritual path.

I would like to emphasize another aspect at this point: upon encountering the Dharma, it is important not to lead a carefree and relaxed life in the arrogant belief that you now are someone special because you are a "Dharma practitioner." Becoming deluded and distracted by the "status" of being a Dharma practitioner, without earnestly engaging in Dharma practice, amounts to squandering the favorable opportunity for genuine spiritual growth. Make sure that you do not develop such an attitude. It sometimes actually happens that individuals who acquire knowledge

15 The "eight freedoms" refer to being free from eight states where there is no opportunity to practice the Buddha Dharma. These are: hells, preta realms, animals, long-lived gods, uncivilized lands, incomplete faculties, wrong views, and living in an era during which no Buddha lived in the world. The "ten opportunities" are grouped into two. The first group concerns circumstantial advantages: a Buddha lived in the world, he has taught the Dharma, the teachings are still flourishing, there are followers of the teachings, and there is assistance from others in one's Dharma practice. The second group concerns individual advantages: being a human being, being born in a land where there is access to the Buddha's teachings, having intact faculties, having not committed very negative deeds, and having faith in the Buddha's teachings.

of the Dharma and engage in reflection and meditation, nevertheless become narrow-minded and conceited if they cultivate a distorted approach towards the Dharma, and consider themselves exceptionally unique. This phenomenon is called the "Dharma pride of arrogance," where one mistakenly believes to know everything better than others. Such pride clouds the mind and presents a significant risk of wasting the precious living conditions of the present. Therefore, I urge you to pay close attention and to prevent the development of any arrogant "Dharma pride" within yourself.

In the past, whether during the time of Buddha Śākyamuni or in subsequent eras, stringent social norms forced the general public to adhere to certain codes of conduct. Today, our societal landscape is markedly different. Many countries prioritize the personal development of individuals, granting them considerable personal freedom to conduct themselves in various ways. Given this increased autonomy, it becomes paramount for individuals to pay meticulous attention to the inner attitudes guiding their behavior. It is crucial to distance oneself from negative thoughts and actions while strengthening beneficial qualities. We should ask ourselves whether our actions are beneficial or not, making a deliberate and responsible choice toward a wholesome direction. This is entirely your own responsibility and is important for all Dharma practitioners, but particularly crucial for those in teaching roles who receive respect and support from others. When the attitude and behavior of teachers are pure, those who support them will accumulate an abundance of merit, and the teachers themselves accumulate merit through practicing pure ethical conduct. Our mind is not hidden to us; we can read our own minds. If we focus on introspection and self-reflection, we will be able to understand our internal processes. For teachers, it is imperative to scrutinize whether their actions align with the Dharma or veer toward potential misuse of the support received. After all, donors contribute because they wish to support the Dharma. In the teachings of the Kadampas and the Shi Je[16], we find the following aspirations: "If we are happy, we offer and dedicate all this to the Buddhas and Bodhisattvas. If we are unhappy, we take on the suffering of all beings; may this lead to the liberation of all beings from the ocean of suffering." Nurturing and cultivating this attitude is of the utmost importance.

I used to have an assistant named Lama Tsultrim Dawa, who passed away some time ago. He was Tibetan and unfamiliar with the Western world, including geography, astronomy, and suchlike. As a result, he held on to the traditional Tibetan worldviews, believing the earth to be a disc and similar ideas. Old Tibet was deeply influenced by religion, with the prevalent custom of sending at least one son from each family to live in the monastery. Consequently, the country had a significant number of monks and lamas. Most of them were devoted Dharma practitioners, but some took advantage of their status as ordained monks.

16 "Shi Je" (Tibetan transliteration: *zhi byed*) literally translates to "pacifying." It is the name of a particular Vajrayāna practice in Tibetan Buddhism founded by Phadampa Sangye at the beginning of the twelfth century; it propagates the practice of the "Chö" (Tibetan transliteration: *gcod*) ritual with the aim to cut through ego clinging in order to pacify suffering.

Lama Tsultrim Dawa once shared a story from his childhood, which he spent in a Karma Kagyu monastery in western Tibet. His teacher, also the abbot of the monastery, received a letter from a Drugpa Kagyu yogi who practiced in seclusion in the region. The letter, sent to various monasteries, described a vision the yogi had during meditation. He explained that he had developed the "eye of stable concentration" and that he saw a distant area in the north, an area very far away from Tibet, with only snow and ice. In this desolate place, the yogi observed birds walking upright like humans, their plumage resembling monks' robes. Seeing these birds suffering in the harsh weather conditions of cold, snow and ice prompted the yogi to contemplate the karmic consequences of such a rebirth. He realized that many former Tibetan monks had been reborn as these birds due to their arrogance and failure to recognize the negative karmic effects, which they brought on themselves by their mistaken belief that they were someone special. In his letter, the yogi urged all monks and lamas to avoid accumulating such negative karma and to practice the Dharma diligently. While the yogi did not identify the birds, I assume they were probably penguins. The overall penguin population may not be extensive. Last year I saw a documentary about penguins and there was talk of a number of four thousand. So there are probably a few ten thousand. And there were not that many monks and nuns in Tibet either. Most of them practiced earnestly anyway, but some apparently made the mistake described above. Interestingly, penguins do bear a resemblance to ordained monks or nuns; yet penguins are skilled swimmers, unlike many Tibetan lamas (laughs).

In any case, the attitude outlined above is crucial: "If I am well, I dedicate this well-being to the Buddhas. If I am in suffering, may the suffering of all beings mature within my own." Similar sentiments can be found in the *Samantabhadra Aspiration Prayers*.[17] There is also a quote from Gampopa in relation to prosperity: "If one is free from clinging, prosperity is a siddhi,"[18] manifesting as a result of merit previously accumulated. So we do not have to reject prosperity as such, but as soon as clinging is involved it becomes a problem.

And here is another piece of advice for those of you who are teaching the Dharma to others: it is crucial not to teach arbitrarily. Individuals seeking your guidance have a sincere desire to learn the Dharma correctly. As mentioned earlier, we currently live in an era marked by prosperity with a significant interest in authentic Dharma. Merely providing general information is not enough.

Ideally, the Dharma should be explained based on the sūtras, the discourses, taught by the Buddha. If this is not feasible, then the teachings should be conveyed using works authored by Buddhist scholars and eminent masters of the past. These śāstras explain the content of the sūtras in great detail. Therefore, teachers should either draw from the sūtras or śāstras as their primary sources, or they can convey Buddhist teachings through engaging stories and

---

17 The *Samantabhadra Aspiration Prayers* are part of the extensive *Avataṃsaka Sūtra*. These aspirations outline the bodhisattvas' attitude and practice.

18 "Siddhi" here refers to special capabilities achieved through spiritual practice.

metaphors. I have adopted the latter approach, as seen in my earlier penguin story, which was aimed to illustrate the causality of actions and their effects.

Of these two approaches, in the context of our discussion on the application of mindfulness, I choose the first and will present the instructions based on a sūtra, using a śāstra as my guide. In my explanations, I will adhere to the principles outlined in this śāstra, as it is my responsibility to do so. In the previous year (2005), I explained Vimalamitra's *Stages of Meditation* (*Gomrim*), focusing on the sequence of calm abiding and deep insight. This year, I will teach the fourfold application of mindfulness. Looking ahead to next year, likely in April, I plan to teach the *Samantabhadra Aspiration Prayers* which is an excerpt from an extensive sūtra. It is advisable to see the current teachings on the fourfold application of mindfulness in the context of the instructions from the preceding year, as the fourfold application of mindfulness encompasses the amalgamation of calm abiding and deep insight.

To commence the explanations on the fourfold application of mindfulness, *The Commentary on Defining the Topics* quotes an introductory question from the sūtra, with which the Buddha initiated this section: "Oh monks, what, in this context, is the fourfold application of mindfulness?"

The śāstra explains that "in this context" refers to the fact that the following instructions are given with regard to a life in the so-called realm of desire or the realm of sensuality.[19] This comprises (1) the six types of *devas* or heavenly beings in the realm of desire, such as the heaven of the thirty-three devas etc.;[20] (2) the *asuras*, that is, the demigods; (3) the humans; (4) the animals; (5) the *pretas* or ghosts; and (6) the hell beings. (...) Basically, the deva worlds in the desire realm are very pleasant states of experience, in which much more well-being and joy is experienced than in a human existence. According to Buddhist description, the human existence comprises

19 The reason why the instructions for the fourfold application of mindfulness are related to the realm of desire or sensuality, including the heavenly beings in the realm of desire, is that in these forms of existence, experience is essentially based on the body and its senses. Hence, practitioners are guided to practice with regard to the body, feelings, the mind, and mental phenomena. Heavenly beings in the two other realms, namely those of form and formlessness, are in a state of mental absorption. In the realm of form, a subtle but more refined body is still experienced, while in the realm of formlessness, there is no bodily experience at all. Therefore, the instructions for the fourfold application of mindfulness are not suitable in the form and formless realms.

20 At this juncture, Shamar Rinpoche listed the six types of deities: They are (1) Parinirmitavaśavartin Devas, (2) Nirmāṇarati Devas, (3) Tuṣita Devas, (4) Yāma Devas, (5) Trāyastrimśa Devas, and (6) Cāturmahārājikakāyika Devas. The Parinirmitavaśavartin Devas are said to be very skillful in mental creativity, projecting their desires into the world. They enjoy their mental power. It is said that the Nirmāṇarati Devas find joy in creating their own beautiful objects and experiences; they live in a world of aesthetic pleasure. The Tuṣita Devas experience much joy and contentment. It is said that Prince Siddhartha, before being reborn as Siddhartha Gautama and becoming the Buddha, spent his last existence in this world. The Yama Devas live in a world of pleasure above the heaven of the Thirty-Three Devas. Their comfort and luxury exceed even those of the previous groups. The Trāyastrimśa Devas inhabit the summit of Mount Sumeru and enjoy a very refined existence. They are ruled by Indra, the king of gods. The Cāturmahārājikakāyika Devas inhabit the lower slopes of Mount Sumeru and guard the four cardinal directions. It is said that they protect the human world.

the human life in the so-called four continents. The reason for the designation "realm of desire or sensuality" is that the body plays a central role, and that strong clinging and physical desire are experienced.[21]

With the phrase "Oh monks," the Buddha primarily directs his words to those practitioners who have renounced worldly life and its activities. Individuals engaged in Buddhist practice as laypeople are referred to as *upāsakas* or *upāsikas*. The Buddha's address encompasses all those in attendance during this instruction, primarily the *bhikṣus*—those who adhere to the 253 vows outlined in the *vinaya*, the scriptures on ethical conduct. He emphasizes that authentic monks are those who diligently engage in the practice of the fourfold application of mindfulness.

The Application of Mindfulness with Regard to the Body

In the śāstra, known as *The Commentary on Defining the Topics*, certain questions are posed to explain the statements made in the sūtra: what does the term "body" mean in this context? How should one understand the act of "contemplating" the body? What does the term "application of mindfulness" entail? What is the purpose of the application of mindfulness?

21 At this point, Shamar Rinpoche did not elaborate on the asuras, animals, hungry ghosts, and hell beings. In principle, these are different realms of perception with varying intensities of suffering and pain. Since beings in these forms of existence are entirely consumed by the effects of their karmic actions and lack the ability for self-reflection, it is almost impossible for them to train their minds and gain insight into the nature of reality—which is what mindfulness practice is about.

What Does the Term "Body" Mean in this Context?

Basically, the application of mindfulness with regard to the body is about contemplating and recognizing both that, and how, we cling to the skandha of the body, or to bodies, as a self or a true being. This clinging refers to all possible types of bodies, which are listed and briefly explained in the following section.

The forthcoming explanation relies on lists found in this context within the Abhidharma. With the aim of comprehensively addressing the subject of "bodies," the śāstra enumerates thirty-five potential types. Today's western biology or natural sciences naturally provide different and precise descriptions of the body. It is worthwhile to compare the extent to which the list presented here is consistent with the contemporary understanding of biology. If western science introduces additional aspects not contained in the thirty-five listed in the śāstra, feel free to include them. The number is not fixed on thirty-five but can easily be extended to forty or more. Nevertheless, in this context, we adhere to the explanations provided by the śāstra. It is important to note that in the discourses and treatises, the sūtras and śāstras, topics are often initially only listed, but not further explained. Based on this, the essential points are then briefly explained and finally this is followed by an explanation as to how to practice meditation in accordance with the topic.

Listing the topics and brief explanation

The thirty-five types of bodies, or all the objects to

which we ascribe a genuine existence:[22]

(1) An inner body: this is one's own body.

(2) An outer body: this is the body of others.

(3) A body endowed with sense faculties: this refers to a form equipped with sensory organs, such as eyes, and the like.

(4) A body devoid of sense faculties: this refers to a form lacking sense organs, exemplified by objects like pillars, houses, walls, and the like. While I am not entirely certain why this is included in the enumeration, the rationale for referring to bodies without sense faculties in this context might be rooted in descriptions of certain painful forms of existence, such as the so-called secondary hells, where self-identification with objects of this nature is mentioned.

(5) A body classified as a living being: this is one that possesses both mind and mental factors. In this context, the term "mind" refers to consciousness, specifically its fundamental cognitive ability, often referred to as the basic mind. The term "mental fac-

22 Here, Shamar Rinpoche initially listed the thirty-five variations of bodies, which are summarized under the heading "bodies," and then, as is done in the śāstra, explained them. For the remaining three topics, "feelings," "the mind" and "mental phenomena," he combined these two sections to avoid unnecessary repetition. Therefore, I have already applied the same principle here and added his brief explanation to the first mention of the thirty-five variations of bodies, which only came later in the oral explanations.

tors" encompasses the various mental formations.[23]

(6) A body not classified as a living being: this is a body that does not possess mind and mental factors.

(7) A body with existential unease:[24] this is the body of all those beings who have not overcome their mental defilements.

(8) A relaxed body: this is the body of noble or realized individuals[25] who have overcome mental defilements.

(9) A body consisting of the causal elements: these are the elements of earth, water, fire, and wind.

(10) A body as an effect, arising from the elements: these are bodies that arise through the interaction of these elements, that is, the five sense organs (eyes, ears, nose, tongue, and skin) serving as the founda-

---

23 In Buddhist psychology, consciousness is precisely explored concerning its functions. In the Abhidharma sources, there is in this context mention of "mental formations" (Sanskrit: *saṃskāra*; Tibetan phonetics: *du je*; Tibetan transliteration: *'du byed*) in this context. Based on the cognitive ability of the "mind" or "consciousness" (Sanskrit: *citta*; Tibetan phonetics: *sem*; Tibetan transliteration: *sems*) through which we perceive rough outlines, mental factors (Sanskrit: *caitta*; Tibetan phonetics: *sem jung*; Tibetan transliteration: *sems byung*) contribute to the specific quality of this experience and thus shape the state of the mind. These mental factors can be positive or negative in nature. Examples include mindfulness, trust, respect, but also desire, aversion, doubt, etc.

24 Existential unease is a translation of the Sanskrit word *dauṣṭhulya* (Tibetan phonetics: *ne ngen len*; Tibetan transliteration: *gnas ngan len*). The idea here is that unsatisfactoriness permeates human existence to such an extent that it is perceived and felt most fundamentally as a situation of affliction, suffering, malaise and powerlessness.

25 The noble or realized individuals refers to arhats and realized bodhisattvas.

tion for sensory perceptions, and their corresponding five sense objects (visual form, sound, smell, taste particles, and tangibles). According to the Yogācāra view,[26] the presence of the five sense organs invariably leads to the experience of their corresponding sense objects. (...) Hence, visual form correlates with the eye sense organ, with its very subtle optic nerve which is compared to a delicate flower. Similar relationships exist between the other sense organs and their respective sense objects. In essence, the sense organs and their corresponding sense objects exist simultaneously, akin to a plant and its fragrance. This type of body is therefore the body which is inseparable from the senses.

(11) A body in the sense of "name": this denotes a form that is imperceptible in a material sense,[27] such as a vow or promise. Body in the sense of "name"

26 Yogācāra refers to one of the two major philosophical perspectives in Mahāyāna Buddhism. It was essentially shaped in the fourth century AD by Maitreya/Asaṅga and Vasubandhu. According to this view, what appears to be an external world is ultimately a projection of the perceiving mind. Perception is understood as something that occurs exclusively in the dualistic mind, which experiences its world due to the effect of deeply ingrained habitual tendencies. Accordingly, beings with similar habitual tendencies experience a similar or even the same world with its sensory objects through their senses.

27 According to the Abhidharma, the "non-physically perceptible forms," along with feelings, perceptions, and formations, belong to the conditioned mental phenomena or dharmas. These "forms" are not material; nevertheless, they are counted among the eleven so-called effective forms (such as the five physical sense objects and the five physical sense faculties). Examples of these non-material forms include mental objects like dream images, experiences of form through meditative concentration, movements through dance/gestures, and vows or promises.

also encompasses the "bodies" of feelings, distinctions, formations, and aspects of consciousness—essentially, everything encapsulated under the term "name." In this context, "name" stands for the fact that we are dealing with mental processes versus matter. Using the earlier example of vows, this concept involves a subtle understanding, representing an innate attachment to a self-identity. This sensed identity, akin to a "promise" or fixation of consciousness, clings to a sense of self or possession, and is here referred to as a body because it is something one grasps or clings to. The term "name" conveys a self-identity linked with the body, embodying the designation "I." Incidentally this is recognized as the foundation of purification in Vajrayāna. (…)[28]

(12) A body in the sense of material form: this pertains to the physical, material skandha of form which is always accompanied by shape and color.

(13) A hell body: this refers to the body of a being in the hell realms.

(14) An animal body: this denotes the body of an animal, such as that of horses, oxen, and others.

(15) A preta body: this signifies the body of hungry ghosts who experience all kinds of sufferings, such as a burning mouth.

(16) A human body: this refers to the body of a human being in one of the four continents.

---

28 Shamar Rinpoche remarked at this point that in all these variations of "body," a distinction is made between specific characteristics and general or generalized characteristics. As he gives detailed explanations on this further down, this short remark has been omitted here.

(17) A deva body: this denotes the body of a heavenly being in the realms of desire, form and formlessness. (…)

(18) A body with cognitive functions: this refers to a body with sense consciousnesses like the eye consciousness and others.

(19) A body without cognitive functions: this points to a body without sense consciousnesses, such as those experiencing the "peak of existence," that is, the highest realm of formlessness. In this state, neither the basic mind nor formations are active; it is a purely mental, subtle condition. However, subliminal clinging to a self remains active, leading these devas to eventually awaken from this state. When their meditative absorption comes to an end, the next rebirth in the cycle of existence will take place. The term "body without cognitive functions" also denotes the meditative absorption of the state of cessation. This refers to arhats who have overcome the stream of deception and thus brought illusion and clinging to a self to an end. This is a level of consciousness in which ignorance is only present as a subtle tendency and is no longer active; they experience neither form nor body and are in a state of meditative absorption.

(20) An inner body: at this point, this denotes a body consisting of flesh, blood, and the like.

(21) An outer body: at this point, this signifies a body without flesh, blood, and the like. (...)[29]

(22) A changed body: this refers to a body after death has occurred, a corpse.

(23) An unchanged body: this signifies the body of a living person.

(24) A female body: this is a body with female sexual organs.

(25) A male body: this is a body with male sexual organs.

(26) A sexless body: this is a body without sexual organs.

(27) The body of friends: these are the bodies of relatives and friends.

(28) The body of enemies: these are the bodies of enemies.

(29) The body of neutral persons: these are the bodies of those who are neither friend nor foe.

(30) A bad body: this refers to an ugly body in color and shape.

(31) A neutral body: this denotes a body that is neither beautiful nor ugly.

(32) A noble body: this means a body that is beautiful in color and shape.

---

29 Shamar Rinpoche asks at this point whether a transparent jellyfish has flesh and blood. If not, something like this could be meant here.

(33) A child body: this refers to the body of a child.

(34) A youthful body: this denotes the body of a young adult who is in the prime of life.

(35) An aging body: this represents the body of an adult undergoing the aging process.

These thirty-five body variations can be summarized in three perspectives:

- The inner body.
- The outer body.
- Both the inner and outer body.

In this context this means the following:

- The inner body refers to one's own body, which is categorized as a living being.
- The outer body refers to material forms which are not viewed as living beings.
- Both the inner and outer body means the bodies of other living beings (considered outer), which are counted as living beings (considered inner). Therefore, these are the bodies of living beings other than oneself.

Another explanation is as follows:

- The inner body is a body equipped with sense organs.
- The outer body is a body lacking sense organs.
- Both the inner and outer body is a body with sense organs (considered inner) existing outside of oneself (considered outer), representing another living being.

An alternative definition would be the following:

- The inner body signifies a form possessing well-being and stages of meditative concentration.
- The outer body represents a form experiencing suffering and lacking stages of meditative concentration.
- Both the inner and outer body are initially endowed with discomfort (considered outer), but as the person enters meditative concentration, it transitions to an experience of well-being (considered inner).

Alternatively, one could explain it as:

- The inner body is a body endowed with consciousness.
- The outer body is a body without consciousness, a corpse, yet it is still classified as a sentient being. For example, when a cow is slaughtered and the meat is consumed, there is a lingering attachment to it being the meat of a cow, not merely a piece of meat.
- Both the inner and outer body are a body that was previously endowed with consciousness (considered inner). When death occurs, this body, now a corpse (considered outer), is no longer endowed with consciousness, therefore it is considered as both an inner and outer body.

Or, one could describe it as follows:

- The inner body encompasses one's own complete bodily appearance, including shape, color, hair, body hair, fingernails, flesh, etc.

- The outer body represents the bodily appearance of others in its entirety, with shape, color, hair, body hair, fingernails, flesh, etc.
- Both the inner and outer body is one's own body (considered inner) after it has become a corpse (considered outer).

What is the purpose of enumerating these different types of body? Essentially, this listing emphasizes the diverse ways in which our consciousness attaches itself to bodies—internally, externally, and both internally and externally. This attachment manifests on both coarse and subtle levels, ranging from temporary to prolonged durations. The purpose of detailing these variations is to bring attention to the mental clinging associated with bodies of all types.

This is a śāstra, a type of treatise known for its comprehensive enumerations, leaving nothing unaddressed. The various descriptions highlight the nuances of holding onto something as a body. For instance, from one's own perspective, one's own body is considered the inner body, while from the viewpoint of others, it becomes an outer, distinct body, signifying that the body is both inner and outer.[30] (...). This is akin to the following example: seen from the perspective of a mouse, the body of a buffalo is large; seen from the perspective of an elephant, however, the buffalo is small—demonstrating the simultaneous largeness and smallness of the same entity.

30 Shamar Rinpoche provided an example: his own body and that of a listener in the audience. Depending on the perspective—from one's own or that of others—it can be considered an inner, outer, or both inner and outer body.

The intention behind these varied descriptions is to emphasize the multifaceted ways in which living beings attribute an essence to bodies and hold onto them in the broadest sense. Each individual has a unique way of holding onto his or her body. When observing the bodies of other living beings, a different form of attachment applies.

Close examination reveals that a body does not inherently possess specific characteristics that are universally real and tangible. If my body truly had its own genuine characteristics, others observing it would also perceive it as "my body" and not as the body of another person. However, from their perspective, "my body" becomes "another body." Hence, the concepts of "mine," "yours," or "others" do not independently and actually exist. Holding onto something as a "body" therefore occurs in our concepts and in our attachment to conventional reality. To help understand this better, the practice of applying mindfulness uses the "body" as the initial object of observation. And to make it easier to understand, this text starts with listing these various modes of holding on to a body.

One postscript to point (5) above (a body that counts as a living being): an intriguing inquiry arises regarding whether tiny dust mites or bacteria fall under this category. Are microorganisms considered living beings? For instance, do the microorganisms inhabiting boiling lava in our ecosystem qualify as living beings? Even in extremely hot places or the coldest zones, like the oldest ice in Greenland, bacteria thrive. While we may perceive them as minuscule, we lack certainty about how they experience themselves as a body. From our perspective, they may seem diminutive, but perhaps, to themselves, they appear colossal.

How to practice accordingly

After listing and briefly explaining the topics, the text proceeds to outline the meditative practice. In this context, the emphasis is on cultivating insight through a three-step process: listening/learning, reflecting, and meditating. Insight emerges from an exploration of both the specific and general or generalized characteristics associated with the various body types.

How Should One Understand the Act of "Contemplating" the Body?

Insight through listening/learning

Through logical thinking or coherent reasoning, we initially grasp that something which we perceive as "a body" lacks a real nature, has no genuine essential characteristics and does not exist independently, in and of itself. A brief excursion into Buddhist epistemology and psychology may aid in gaining a more precise understanding of this. To present a clear picture of our perceptual processes, Buddhist epistemology first of all differentiates between the so-called specific characteristic and the general or generalizing characteristic. Things are then examined from these two perspectives.

The specific characteristic is what a thing is in itself, irrespective of the generalizing concept it is labeled with. For instance, in the case of the body, it is the body as such; ultimately, the specific characteristics are the finest components of the body. These are specific characteristics in that they are not mixed with something else, that is, not combined with concepts and attributions. However, our comprehension of it arises through the generalizing characteristic. In the context of Buddhist epistemology, this implies that in our perception, we abstract, generalize, and put a name on it. Therefore, when we use the term "body," we are referring to bodies in the broadest sense. Using the term "body" in a generalizing way allows us to infer and understand all bodies of all living beings. The conceptual imputation, where we attribute something to the specific characteristic in our imagination and the accompanying holding onto it, constitutes the generalizing characteristic. Hence, the specific and the generalizing characteristics differ from each other.

The specific characteristic is the thing itself, while the generalizing characteristic is the conceptual way we relate to things. The generalizing characteristic encompasses our mental processes where we form coherent mental images, recognize meanings, and attribute associations from numerous sensory impressions. For example, when we see another person, in the initial moment, we simply perceive an appearance. Only in the subsequent moments of this perceptual process do we identify this appearance with the body of a specific person. We do so through the process of generalizing and attributing. In the first moment of this rapidly occurring perceptual process, we perceive only the body itself, the specific thing, without connecting it with a concept or an idea. The naming, understanding, and the like occur in the subsequent thought processing. Only with the generalizing characteristics do we make the corresponding distinction and assign, for example, the term "the body of..." to it. It is, therefore, an abstraction. The term or concept of "body" is thus a mental process which helps us relate to bodies in general. Yet, it is merely an idea and therefore not identical with the specific characteristic, the thing itself.

As long as we do not differentiate between these specific and the generalizing characteristics, we inevitably cling to our concept of the body as our true identity in the sense of "my" actual body. In other words, we take the generalizing characteristic for the specific characteristic and experience this as "I" or "mine." The specific characteristic, that is, the body itself ultimately consists of miniscule and constantly changing components. With the generalizing characteristic and thus the term "my body," we merge all these components into a mental image or mental representation of the object and mistake this abstraction as our actual body. Holding on to this mistaken perception inevitably leads to a differentiation between our body and that of others. Through our notions of the generalizing type described above, our own body and that of others thus gain a reality they do not inherently possess—after all, the body is merely a constantly changing accumulation of cells or fine particles. In doing so, we mistake the body, which is simply the specific characteristic and thus not an "I" or "mine," as a consistent self, as something special, as a unified whole, and so on. In our perception, this process of generalizing or abstracting that we add to the specific characteristic, immediately follows the first moments of experiencing something, when the perceived thing itself, the specific characteristic, is grasped directly and free from concepts. It is important to understand these principles. Through listening to and learning about these principles, you develop insight as it unfolds from learning.

Insight through reflecting

Once you have comprehended the above through logical thinking, the subsequent step is to independently and profoundly explore and analyze it. This process of reflection will enable you to become certain that what has been described above holds true. It is up to you to engage in these reflections and to decide how thoroughly you want to delve into them. What is the potential result of this reflection? It can lead us to the understanding that the body, as commonly experienced, lacks any inherent reality. While it cannot be fully conveyed in words, it involves essentially the following: you will on the one hand come to comprehend that the body is a thing with its perishable substance, functionality, and so on, and on the other hand that there is an ongoing clinging to the body as a complete entity. Concerning one's own body, this clinging manifests as a consistent experience of "I" and "mine." The latter is the perspective of generalizing ideas that occur in the consciousness, specifically regarding the body and its substance.

By accurately distinguishing and exploring these two perspectives—the specific and the generalizing characteristics—a certainty within you will arise that this body is not actually real. You will understand that the consciousness simply clings to an internal image, an idea, a concept. You will comprehend that your experience of “I” and “mine” in this context is mistaken because fundamentally there is no real reference point for it. A collection of constantly changing cells cannot constitute a solid foundation. You will eventually understand all of this precisely. This is the insight that emerges from reflection, from a discerning exploration.

Insight through meditating

Once you have gained insight developed through reflecting, the next step is to become increasingly familiar with what you have understood. You will achieve this by consistently dwelling upon the acquired insight, in other words, through meditation. The way *how* you maintain this understanding in your meditative state naturally emerges from the understanding described above.

So, once you have studied this matter and cultivated your insight through learning, you should contemplate it in depth in order to also develop your insight through reflection. The emphasis here is not on debating this with others but on genuinely finding this out through personal effort. Debates often complicate matters because too much is said and the dynamics of winners and losers in a discussion come into play. Even if it is not a question of winning or losing a debate, there is certainly too much talk, which contributes to distraction. However, if you take the time to familiarize yourself with this understanding, to examine and explore this matter in depth on your own, you will develop a clear understanding of the topic. You will comprehend how you cling to the "body" as an identity and how the concepts of holding onto "I" and "mine" operate within you. It will genuinely become clear to you that all of this does not really exist. This understanding goes far beyond what can be achieved by merely hearing or reading explanations or descriptions about it. By taking the time to carry out an in-depth exploration as described above you will naturally know how to absorb yourself in meditation. Consequently, insight born from meditation will grow in you. As you realize that the body has no inherent nature, your attachment to the body as a self will gradually dissolve. Thus, you will develop insight from meditation, revealing the nature of things, the true nature of the ground.

Water as a metaphor for insight

This process of developing insight through meditation can be compared to water originating from a spring. The insight gained from listening/learning serves as the riverbed; it is not the water itself. By listening/learning, you operate solely within the realm of concepts and ideas. While they point you in the right direction, they do not constitute the actual experience. Staying with the metaphor, ideas do not have the nature of water. The insight gained through reflection corresponds to the river emanating from the spring and coursing along the riverbed. The insight from meditation is comparable with the sea: the river's water has reached and merged with the ocean. At this stage, you experience immediately and directly the deep and expansive insight that arises only through meditation.

Brief summary

To summarize, in the śāstra, a threefold development of insight has been described: (1) how a certain insight from learning arises initially through listening, (2) how it deepens through reflection or contemplation, and (3) how it then naturally leads to the fruit of being able to remain evenly in this view, which in turn will lead to the insight of meditation.

Regarding the insight that arises from these three—listening/learning, reflecting, and meditating—the śāstra provides precise instructions concerning the body as the initial reference point. When it comes to the application of mindfulness to feelings, mind, and mental phenomena, these are not explained again in detail in the śāstra because their approach should follow the same principle described above in relation to the body. It is therefore important that you understand the fundamental approach based on the body and apply it similarly to feelings, the mind, and mental phenomena.

What Does the Term "Application of Mindfulness" Entail?

The application of mindfulness in the context of the body means being utterly attentive while listening/learning, reflecting, and meditating specifically directed toward the body. It involves maintaining focus on the subject without losing attention. In the previous section details concerning the contemplation with regard to the body and its specific and generalizing characteristics were explained. These same principles should be applied to the other focal points: feelings, the mind, and mental phenomena.

In essence, "applying mindfulness" involves recalling the perspectives explained above, that is, maintaining a state of "being present," and ensuring that the gained insight is not forgotten.

What is the Purpose of the Application of Mindfulness?

The application of mindfulness serves the purpose of guarding against distraction and restlessness, preventing mental defilements, and fostering precise focus. In connection with the body, this is explained as follows:

- Applying mindfulness serves as protection against forgetting the instructions on how to observe the body. It acts as a safeguard against distraction and restlessness, whether triggered by physical sensory perceptions or purely mental processes.
- Applying mindfulness prevents mental defilements concerning the body; the mind is clear and attentive. This also entails not being obsessively absorbed or tense when contemplating the features of the body. An example of practicing obsessively or tensely is to continually think, "the body does not exist, the body does not exist," or to constantly repeat "empty, empty, empty". This would amount to an excessive clinging to such ideas.
- Applying mindfulness ensures precise focus and allows for a constant and accurate deepening of the contemplation with regard to the body. This involves maintaining a continu-

ous observation of the topic without drifting away, akin to the flow of a river. This embodies the one-pointed quality of calm abiding.

Now, let us delve into a more detailed exploration of the practice of applying mindfulness with regard to the "inner body" based on the śāstra's instructions:

The inner body—scrutinizing its specific and generalizing/general characteristics

The exploration of the inner body begins with an examination of the specific characteristics of one's own body: take a close look at what constitutes your body, exploring all the components down to the finest particles. One possible way of observing the body, which is typically perceived as a unified whole, is to mentally deconstruct it: there is the head, the hands, the legs, and so on. This scrutiny illuminates that none of these components possess an intrinsically real nature. Hence, the body lacks any real essential characteristics.

Indirectly, it becomes evident that our generalizing idea or the generalizing characteristic concerning the body does not align with the specific characteristic of the body. We harbor a generalized notion of a body, wherein we take all these components as *one* body and mistakenly believe this to constitute our actual body. In this way we are deluded by way of generalizing.

Seeing clearly by virtue of the antidote and abiding in this understanding

In this meditation, you engage in two key aspects as delineated in the śāstra: "Gain clarity through applying the antidote and abide in this understanding, having overcome what opposes it."

In this context, the antidote is insight, enabling us to see clearly and therefore being able to discern the specific and general characteristics in detail. This functions as a remedy against the opposing influence of deception, embodied in desires, aversions, and similar inclinations, which tend to prompt attachment or rejection. Having understood this, you should then remain in this insight.

Insight acts as an antidote to your deception because, through insight, you clearly understand that the characteristics or qualities attributed to objects do not truly belong to them. Your deception naturally dissolves with this insight. All these deceptive tendencies only exist in your own mental constructs, which are then projected onto things. Reflection results in a precise comprehension of the specific and generalizing characteristics related to your own body. By consistently abiding in meditation based on this understanding, you overcome desires associated with the body and similar attachments. Consequently, the sūtra emphasizes that practitioners are "free from desire" or "liberated from worldly cravings." Likewise, the experience of rejecting ceases, leading to a tranquil mind. Therefore, the sūtra indicates that the "mind is free from discomfort." This insight unfolds through the stages of listening/learning, reflecting, and meditating.

The specific characteristic of the body is the body as such, independent of any designation. It comprises countless finest particles, constituting an amalgamation of cells in constant flux. At the level of these individual particles, no enduring entity exists, no solid body—only perpetual change. Consequently, the specific characteristic of the body lies in its incessant change. In short, the specific characteristic of the body is subtle impermanence.

The generalizing characteristic, on the other hand, involves attributing a permanent quality to this ever-changing accumulation of cells, labeling it a body and experiencing it as a *unique* body, *my* body. By erroneously regarding the body as something permanent, real, and unique, you misinterpret the specific characteristic of the body, that is, its subtle impermanence. Once you comprehend this, it becomes evident that the general characteristic of the body is impermanence. This principle holds true for each and every body. Clinging to the notion of permanence inevitably leads to suffering. Insight, developed by understanding the body's impermanence, essencelessness, and emptiness dissolves this clinging and the suffering associated with it. These general characteristics—that is, impermanence, essencelessness, and emptiness—apply to all bodies.[31] Once you have achieved a precise understanding of the specific as well as the generalizing and general characteristics through listening/learning and reflecting, meditation will pave the way for the arising of profound insight.

The effect of practicing mindfulness

The application of mindfulness is geared toward recognizing impermanence, suffering, emptiness, and essencelessness.

Impermanence: Impermanence can be differentiated between gross and subtle. Gross impermanence is how we usually perceive death, as a break in continuity, thinking that the body ceases to be alive all of a sudden, just like a pot that has been smashed with a hammer. However, even throughout life, the body undergoes constant subtle change, moment by moment. This is the subtle aspect of impermanence.

31 As mentioned earlier, in the context of the fourfold application of mindfulness, the term "general characteristic" does not only refer to a "generalizing characteristic" but is primarily used to denote what is common to all bodies, feelings, the mind, and mental phenomena alike: they are impermanent, essenceless, and empty, and clinging to them leads to suffering. Here is a relevant quote from Vasubandhu's *Abhidharma Treasury* and a commentary by the Ninth Karmapa: "The 'specific characteristics' with regard to the body are that it consists of the basic elements and physical matter that arise from it; with regard to feelings, that experiences take place; with regard to the mind, that something is apprehended; and with regard to mental phenomena, these are the phenomena of distinctions, formation, and the unconditioned, which are not already contained in the other three, namely the body, feelings, and the mind. The 'general characteristic' is that everything conditioned is impermanent, impure phenomena always involve suffering, and all phenomena are empty and without identity."

It is the fact that the sum of finest particles, which we collectively generalize as "bodies," constantly change; not a single cell of the body is ever static. All things, including the conditioned body, change in terms of their finest building blocks from moment to moment, with minute particles constantly disintegrating and renewing themselves.

Suffering: Attributing permanence to the body inevitably leads to suffering, which manifests in various forms: (1) the suffering of suffering, that is to say, pain, (2) the suffering of change, and (3) the ever-present suffering of conditioned existence. As an example of the suffering of suffering, consider the pain experienced by bacteria living in extreme heat, assuming we can attribute a sense of pain to them. The suffering of change becomes apparent when, for instance, we lose our good health due to severe illness. The ever-present suffering of conditioned existence consists in clinging to our experiences. As long as we cling to the body as representing our felt identity, this clinging already encompasses suffering because it forms the basis of the first two types of suffering. Without this existential suffering, this holding onto the experience, there would be no suffering of suffering or suffering of change. Realized beings, understanding emptiness and essencelessness, comprehend this third type of suffering and empathize with the pain others feel. While they are free from clinging and do not personally suffer, their sensitivity towards the pain of others is comparable to having a hair in one's eye. Ordinary beings experience the ever-present suffering of conditioned existence, but they often fail to understand it. This lack of awareness is akin to having a hair on the palm of our hands, which we ordinarily would not even notice. Consequently, those not engaged in the contemplation explained above remain unaware of the remedies to counteract this suffering, leading to the perpetuation of the suffering of suffering and the suffering of change.

Emptiness: This term denotes the inherent nature of all phenomena as being empty. The body is composed of finest particles, which, in turn, prove to be non-existent in reality. Therefore, the inner body, that is to say, one's own body, lacks an autonomous, independent inherent nature. The same principle applies to every moment of consciousness. By consciousness, we refer to the apparent continuity between past, present, and future moments of experience, assembling them in our perception as a coherent mental image. However, since the present moment of consciousness is proven not to be real, the same naturally applies to all other past and future moments of consciousness. As consciousness lacks an autonomous, independent inherent nature, it is devoid of a real essence. Hence, emptiness is the true nature of the mind.

Essencelessness: This term signifies the recognition of emptiness, the insight that brings an end to the habitual clinging to an attributed identity or reality. With the aid of meditation, we can transform our correct understanding which we have developed through reflection into a direct, immediate experience.

In the practice of mindfulness, the initial focus involves contemplating your own body before extending this awareness to other bodies. Gradually, this practice involves focusing on the various forms of clinging to bodies as mentioned earlier.

In relation to the "inner body", the progress of the practice, which entails developing insight through listening, reflecting, and meditating on the specific and generalizing/general characteristics, has now been comprehensively described. For the other reference points—such as other bodies, feelings, the mind, and mental phenomena—the śāstra's instructions are to apply the same method as with the "inner body." Therefore, it is essential to adjust the progress of contemplation and exploration accordingly, thereby honing the skill of contemplation, that is to say of *samādhi* or meditative absorption.

The Application of Mindfulness with Regard to Feelings

The sūtra refers to "inner and outer, and both inner and outer feelings." The term "feelings" comprises pleasant, unpleasant, and neutral feelings; the latter are neither pleasant nor unpleasant. Feelings can be more closely associated with the body or with the consciousness. Body feelings are mainly experienced in the realms of desire and to some extent also in the deva realms of form. Mental feelings, essentially denoting feelings associated with meditative absorption, prevail in the deva realms of form and formlessness. In a broader sense, mental feelings are those arising from meditative absorption.

Listing the topics and brief explanation

(1) Pleasant feelings are those perceived as physically and mentally comforting and supportive.

(2) Unpleasant feelings are those that feel painful and hurtful.

(3) Neutral feeling are those that are neither pleasant nor painful, and therefore neutral.

Feelings connected with the senses, that is, sight, hearing, smell, taste, and touch, are physical feelings. In contrast, feelings felt *only* in the mind-consciousness are mental feelings. The latter are a matter of genuine meditative absorption, that is, *dhyāna*, and thus primarily pertain to the deva realms of form and formlessness.

Feelings can be associated with agitation or with calmness. Agitation refers to a mental state disturbed by its defilements. In short, all feelings which are part of the three realms of cyclic existence and involve attachment to the five sense objects are based on craving. Therefore, they are always associated with more or less agitation. The feelings of realized individuals from the path of seeing onwards are free from agitation in a state which is matching the peace of *nirvāṇa*. In their case, physical feelings simply arise from the interplay of the elements of earth, water, fire, and wind; they are free from desire.

How to practice accordingly

In the practice of applying mindfulness with regard to feelings, you proceed in the same way as explained for the inner body:

- Inner feelings: these are experiences occurring within one's own five aggregates, that is, form/matter, feelings, distinctions/perception, formations, and consciousness. Be mindful of them and engage in contemplation.

- Outer feelings: these arise in connection with outer objects of perception, that is, with inanimate objects, such as visual forms, sounds, smells, taste particles, and touch. Be aware of them and contemplate.
- Both inner and outer feelings: these arise from interactions with other living beings. Be mindful of them and contemplate. From a personal standpoint, they are outer; from the perspective of others involved, they are inner feelings.

In meditative absorption, you direct your attention to these different aspects and thus train yourself in various samādhis, that is, in states of absorption; it is therefore a training in samādhi skills.

Just as explained before, begin by concentrating on your own five aggregates and the feelings experienced during your contemplation. Then shift your attention to the perception of visual forms, sounds, smells, tastes, and tangible things, along with the feelings you are undergoing during your contemplation. Afterward, direct your attention to other individuals and how feelings arise in you when thinking of other individuals. By training in the samādhi of the application of mindfulness, you will eventually be able to understand the specific characteristic of feelings, that is, that we experience or feel something. You should also observe how feelings continuously change from moment to moment, realizing that their inherent nature is emptiness which in turn is their general characteristic. Practicing mindfulness with these contemplations is a way of training in samādhi.

The three types of feelings

So, here we are dealing with the three types of feelings: unpleasant, pleasant, and neutral feelings. Unpleasant ones are feelings of the suffering of suffering, and are painful. As all pleasant feelings are continually subject to change they are fundamentally unpleasant as well; these are the feelings of the suffering of change. Feelings neither pleasant nor unpleasant represent the ever-present suffering of conditioned existence and are perceived as neutral, as neither painful nor pleasant; nevertheless, it is a type of suffering, namely the suffering of clinging to a self which leads to the restless mind states of conditioned existence.

The first step is that you correctly understand this by listening and learning, which will lead to a first level of insight. Deep reflection will sharpen your understanding; you will realize more clearly that feelings, regardless of their nature or whatever you feel, lack an inherent nature. You will also comprehend that neither the suffering experienced by an individual, nor consequently its experiencer—the consciousness of that individual—have an inherent nature. Finally, through meditation, your mind will undergo a tangible transformation, achieving a direct knowing. This concludes the application of mindfulness regarding feelings and their true nature.

The Application of Mindfulness with Regard to the Mind

In the śāstra, twenty mental states are outlined. The initial six delineate the three mental defilements of desire, aversion, and dullness. It is essential to recognize them when they arise. Similarly, when you have successfully applied the corresponding antidotes, leading to a mental state free from these afflictions, be mindful of this freedom from mental defilements.

Listing the topics and brief explanation

(1) A mind of desire: this is a mental state experienced by samsaric beings in the three realms, relating to desired things like possessions and wealth. Beings are ensnared by their desire and act accordingly.

(2) A mind free from desire: this is a mental state experienced on the path of the Noble Ones, especially starting with the path of seeing;[32] on this stage, practitioners see reality directly. Desire is only subtly present as a tendency; these beings are not influenced by it and do not act accordingly.

32 The "path of seeing" is one of the five paths of a practitioner's spiritual accomplishments. The first from among these five paths is the one of accumulation; the second is the path of unification or preparation; the third is the path of seeing, the fourth is the path of cultivation, and the fifth is the path of no-more-learning. The third, that is, the path of seeing, is identical with the first *bhūmi*, that is, the first "level," with a direct realization of absolute reality. From this point onward, bodhisattvas are said to not be propelled into further rebirths in cyclic existence through the power of their craving, emotional defilements and karma. Rather, they take rebirth through their strong and pure aspiration to be of benefit to sentient beings.

(3) A mind of aversion: this is a mental state experienced by samsaric beings in the three realms concerning things they reject. Beings are subject to it and act accordingly.

(4) A mind free from aversion: this is a mental state experienced on the path of the Noble Ones, especially starting with the path of seeing; on this stage, practitioners see reality directly. Aversion is only subliminally present as a tendency; these beings are not influenced by it and do not act accordingly.

(5) A mind of dullness: this is a mental state experienced by samsaric beings. Beings are subject to it and act accordingly.

(6) A mind free from dullness: This is a mental state experienced on the path of the Noble Ones, especially starting with the path of seeing; on this stage, practitioners see reality directly. Dullness is only subliminally present as a tendency; these beings are not influenced by it and do not act accordingly.

Three of these six mental states outlined above are mental defilements or *kleśas*. Beings are influenced by them and act accordingly; these are to be abandoned. The other three represent the remedies on the path and should be practiced.

(7) A concentrated mind: this is a mental state dwelling within itself; shiné or calm abiding.

(8) A distracted mind: this is a mental state following sense objects and not remaining in a calm state.

(9) A depressed mind: this is a mental state of drowsiness and lethargy.

(10) A joyfully inspired, sublime, and encouraged mind: this is a mental state that clears away drowsiness and lethargy. It is the joy arising from the samādhi of deep insight and its discerning knowing.

(11) A wild, restless mind: this is a mental state that arises when the joyfully inspired mental state is lost, and distraction sets in.

(12) A mind free from wildness and restlessness: this is a mental state arising when lethargy and restlessness are overcome, and the mind remains imperturbable.

(13) A peaceful mind: this is a mental state when hindrances like drowsiness/dullness, remorse, doubt, and the like, have been overcome. It is attained at the end of the path of unification.

(14) A non-peaceful mind: this is a mental state when hindrances have not been overcome.

(15) A mind that remains perfectly balanced: this is a mental state dwelling in the four dhyānas, that is, the four stages of genuine mental tranquility. It is necessary to develop the four dhyānas in order to be able to achieve true calm abiding and deep insight. The four dhyānas progressively become subtler and calmer, with the fourth stage being completely tranquil. Just like the fourfold applications of mindfulness, the four dhyāna stages can be systematically learned and practiced.

(16) A mind not perfectly balanced: this is a mental state not dwelling in any of the four dhyānas.

(17) A mind very familiar with the path of meditation: this is a mental state that has become very familiar with one of the four dhyānas, genuine meditative absorptions, and is thus able to dwell in it for a long time. Described here is a mind that has mastered this and has therefore developed extraordinary abilities such as clairvoyance, miraculous powers, etc., which can arise as a result. This is an important point because it is possible to attain the actual dhyāna but not continue to practice it.

(18) A mind not very familiar with the path of meditation: this is a mental state that has attained the four dhyānas or some of them and has become familiar with them but, not having mastered them entirely, the extraordinary abilities that could otherwise arise as a result have not been developed.

(19) A mind that has become liberated through utmost familiarity with the practice: this is a mental state attained through intensive meditation practice. The four dhyānas of calm abiding have been attained, and the samādhi of deep insight has been practiced. As a result, kleśas have been completely purified, and the mind is perfectly pure.

(20) A mind that has not become liberated through utmost familiarity with the practice: this is a mental state in which some but not all kleśas have been purified.

These twenty mental states can be further divided into three categories:

- The inner mind: this pertains to one's own mind, encompassing the cognitive faculty (basic mind) and mental factors.
- The outer mind: this refers to a mental state triggered by an external factor that is not a living being, such as a visual form.
- Both the inner and outer mind: this involves a mental state triggered by another living being.

How to engage in the practice accordingly

In the practice of mindfulness concerning the mind, you employ the same approach as detailed in relation to the inner body.

Contemplating the mind involves observing, understanding, and experiencing how the mind and its accompanying mental factors undergo constant change from moment to moment. You observe the dynamic nature of the mind, recognizing that it is never static and consistently in flux.

Through this firsthand experience, you come to realize that there is no enduring and unchanging mind that can serve as a genuine basis for self-identification. Simultaneously, you understand that the subjective aspect—the tendency to cling to a sense of self—does not exist in its own right. This insight leads to liberation from desires and similar attachments. Such understanding is an insight cultivated through reflection and meditation, progressively deepening through the latter and ultimately reaching a state of perfection.

The Application of Mindfulness with Regard to Mental Phenomena (Dharmas)

This practice bears resemblance to the third one, that is, the application of mindfulness with regard to the mind. In this context, "dharma" is defined as that which is experienced by the mind-consciousness. It encompasses everything that can be experienced. Consequently, it pertains once again to the twenty mental states delineated earlier, as these constitute what is experienced. Classified as mental phenomena, they are further divided into ten negative dharmas and ten positive dharmas.

To clarify the term "dharma" further: in this context, it does not denote the Dharma within the framework of the Three Jewels or the Buddha's teachings. The Sanskrit term "dharma" carries a multitude of meanings, ranging from Buddhist practice as a wholesome and liberating way to live life to encompassing various philosophical connotations. Thus, "dharma" can mean: (1) that which is experienced, (2) the path, (3) nirvāṇa, (4) the object of mind-consciousness, (5) wholesome or beneficial, (6) life, (7) the Buddha's teachings, (8) the future that will occur, and (9) religion. In the context of the fourfold application of mindfulness, "dharma" encompasses all these meanings. In essence, "dharma" here represents all phenomena of saṃsāra and nirvāṇa, encapsulating everything that can be experienced.

Listing the topics and brief explanation

The twenty dharmas, categorized as negative and positive mental phenomena, are as follows:

(1) Craving: involves clinging to forms and other sense objects.

(2) Tamed craving: involves meditation on non-beauty.

(3) Aversion: involves feeling anger towards enemies, and the like.

(4) Tamed aversion: involves developing loving-kindness as an antidote to aversion.

(5) Dullness/delusion: involves not understanding actions and their consequences.

(6) Tamed dullness/delusion: involves insight that understands the specific and general characteristics of all things and thereby understands karma and its workings.

(7) Concentration: this is a mind that dwells inwardly in one-pointedness.

(8) Distraction: this is a mind that is influenced by sensory objects.

(9) Sloth: this is a mind dampened by drowsiness and lethargy.

(10) Joyful elevation: this is the effect of dhyāna, a mental state in which, due to contemplating the qualities of the Tathāgata, dullness and lethargy have cleared.

(11) Restlessness: this is a mind that loses the joyful elevated mental state and wanders.

(12) Non-restlessness: this is a mind that has over-

come sloth and restlessness and remains imperturbable.

(13) Peace: this is a mind free from hindrances such as drowsiness/dullness, remorse, doubt, and the like.

(14) Non-peace: this is a mind that has not freed itself from hindrances.

(15) True equanimity: this is a mind that dwells balanced in the first, second, third, or fourth dhyāna.

(16) Non-equanimity: this is a mind that does not dwell balanced in the first, second, third, or fourth dhyāna.

(17) Utmost familiarity with the path of meditation: this is present when the path of the Noble Ones has been attained through meditation.

(18) No utmost familiarity with the path: this is the case when the path of the Noble Ones has not been attained through meditation.

(19) Freedom through utmost familiarity with the practice of meditation: this is the case when, through intensive meditation, all mental defilements of the three realms have been overcome and do not arise again.

(20) Non-freedom through utmost familiarity with the practice of meditation: this is the case when, due to a lack of intensive meditation, not all mental defilements have been overcome.

These twenty mental phenomena can also be classified into the following three categories:

- o Internal phenomena: mental phenomena that arise within ourselves.
- o External phenomena: mental phenomena that arise within us triggered by something external that is not a living being.
- o Both internal and external phenomena: mental phenomena that arise within us triggered by other living beings.

As explained above, the focus is on training yourselves in samādhi so that you direct the mind slightly differently towards the beneficial and thus cultivate states of meditative absorption.

If the ten negative mental phenomena predominate the mind—that is, if these are what you experience—it is a mental state with defilements. Being free from these is a mind that experiences the ten wholesome mental phenomena. The latter does not represent a separate mental state, but rather denotes the state of purity, cleansed from the mental defilements, that is, the ten negative states.

How to engage in the practice accordingly

The application of mindfulness with regard to mental phenomena, known as dharmas, involves recognizing these mind states as unreal and aiming to attain freedom from any grasping.

Once again, the practice involves engaging in listening and learning, reflecting, and meditating in order to cultivate the three levels of insight. Ultimately, this process leads to the realization of selflessness. Recognizing selflessness, or the absence of essence, entails letting go of the attachment to the self. Fundamentally, the self has never been more than a mental defilement. The complete understanding of this dissolves your misconception with regard to the self. It is crucial to comprehend that the self has not been eliminated or eradicated and an entity of selflessness or an absence of essence has been attained. There never was such a self, a true being. The experience of self was merely an illusion. The insight gained from meditation is free from this deception and, therefore, cognizant of the true nature of all phenomena—their *dharmatā*.

At the beginning, when applying mindfulness with regard to the inner body, we looked at the three following aspects:

- Guarding against distraction and restlessness: this means that we keep up a sustained focus and avoid forgetting the instructions.
- Preventing mental defilements: this means that we avoid being overwhelmed by afflictions, staying alert and being clear.
- Ensuring that we maintain a precise focus: this means to continuously practice in even-minded absorption, that is, in deep samādhi.

All three aspects should equally be practiced, in the current context as well as with regard to the other reference points.

The Five Aspects of the Application of Mindfulness

In the upcoming section, the fourfold application of mindfulness is further explained, focusing on the following five aspects: (1) the reference points, (2) the essence, (3) the companions, (4) the meditation practice, and (5) the fruition of meditation practice. These five aspects are equally applicable to the other components of the Thirty-seven Factors Conducive to Awakening. I hope that, in the future, you will be able to explore the additional aspects of the thirty-seven factors as well.

The Reference Points

The reference points of the fourfold application of mindfulness are the body, feelings, the mind, and dharmas, or mental phenomena. We can also say that in practice, we contemplate the following:

- the support on which the experience of self occurs—namely, the body;
- all experiences, sensations, based on the identification with the body—namely, feelings;
- the experiencer in whom the experience of a self takes place—namely, the mind, and
- all that the mind experiences—namely, the dharmas or mental phenomena. These may be associated with mental defilements in the realm of saṃsāra, or with the process of purification.

Most ordinary individuals, whose perception is characterized by a distorted experience, perceive their body with its sensory abilities as the foundation for self-identification, designating it as "my body." Building upon this, they experience pleasant, unpleasant, and neutral feelings. The mind serves as the experiencer of these feelings, constituting consciousness. When the mind—driven by pleasant, unpleasant, or neutral feelings—experiences desire, anger, dullness, pride, envy, and similar emotions, it is subject to mental defilements. If, on the other hand, the mind engages in "remedies" like confidence, joyful perseverance, meditative concentration, insight, and the like, it is connected with processes of purification. It is the mind that experiences both aspects. Therefore, they are categorized as mental phenomena that comprise everything that can be perceived.

Practicing mindfulness with a correct understanding of these four reference points—the body, feelings, the mind, and mental phenomena—and progressively recognizing and experiencing their nature or mode of being, while consistently abiding in this insight, constitutes the application of mindfulness by means of these four reference points.

The Nature

The fourfold application of mindfulness concerning the body, and so forth, comprises deep insight and calm abiding, that is to say, lhagthong (*vipaśyanā*) and shiné (śamatha). The expression "contemplating" the body, etc. underscores the dimension of deep insight. Simultaneously, the phrase "continuous application of mindfulness," highlights the aspect of calm abiding and means to constantly remain in insight.

The Companions

The practice of the fourfold application of mindfulness requires supportive, wholesome mental factors. Therefore, in order for us to be able to practice mindfulness, which entails not forgetting the instructions and remedies and immediately applying them when necessary, we also need to cultivate the support of other factors such as right intention, joyful perseverance, meditative concentration, insight, and the like. Without these wholesome factors, it is not possible to develop the application of mindfulness in the sense described above.

The Meditation Practice

The actual training in meditation entails delving into the specific and generalizing or general characteristics of the body, feelings, the mind, and mental phenomena. Practicing involves thoroughly exploring these characteristics and gaining familiarity with them in meditative concentration. This exploration encompasses all levels—internal, external, and both internal and external. As you progress in your practice, you come to recognize that nothing whatsoever possesses an inherent existence. You directly and immediately perceive the true nature of all phenomena.

The Fruition of Meditation Practice

The fruition of the meditation practice involves (1) overcoming the four types of distorted experiences, (2) gaining access to the Four Noble Truths, and (3) liberating oneself from suffering that is associated with the body, feelings, the mind, and mental phenomena.

Overcoming distorted experiences

In this section, four types of distorted experiences are identified, namely, the perception of things as pure, joyful, permanent, and possessing a self or essence.

Contemplating the body aids in overcoming the distorted experience of clinging to the body as inherently pure, joyful, permanent, and possessing a self or essence. You will come to understand that the body is impure, painful, impermanent, and self- or essenceless. The expression "impure versus pure" does not carry the connotation that anything to do with the body is something which is morally reprehensible. It rather emphasizes the understanding that all suffering is experienced based on the body. The objective of the practice is therefore not to reject or destroy the body but to overcome our attachment to it. As long as attachment to the body persists, suffering remains inevitable. This is because the four distorted types of experience manifest themselves in selfishness, pride, and suchlike which in turn lead to suffering. Engaging in mindfulness with regard to the body and the other aspects prepares the ground for a correct understanding of the nature of the body, feelings, the mind, and mental phenomena. This understanding helps to dissolve distorted clinging, which in turn brings suffering to an end.

The Buddha recommended this contemplation with regard to the body primarily to counteract the distorted experience of perceiving what is actually impure as pure. The contemplation on feelings mainly addresses the distorted experience of regarding suffering as something joyful and acknowledging that, after all, all feelings, even pleasant and neutral ones, are connected with the three types of suffering. He taught the contemplation with regard to the mind primarily to counteract the distorted experience of perceiving what is impermanent as something permanent. If you recognize the momentary nature of the mind, that perceptions change from moment to moment and never remain the same, you will find access to the mind's true mode of being. This in turn will reduce the clinging to the mind as something that is constant and possesses its own identity. The Buddha taught the contemplation with regard to mental phenomena mainly to counteract the distorted experience of perceiving what is essenceless as something constituting a self or essence. Through this contemplation, you will come to recognize the true nature of all experiences.

Gaining Access to the Four Noble Truths

By practicing mindfulness with regard to the body, you will gain an understanding of the first aspect of the Four Noble Truths, the truth of suffering, because you will clearly perceive that the body is inherently subject to afflictions such as illness, aging, and death. You will recognize that various sufferings in relation to the body are inevitable. Although the Buddha was a prince and privileged, with extremely comfortable living conditions, through the application of mindfulness with regard to the body he realized that his life was full of suffering and insubstantial. Life may be beautiful at times, but, as mentioned above, it is always permeated with the existential suffering which is inseparable from our existence. The suffering of change and the suffering of suffering in the form of birth, aging, illness, and death can only manifest on the basis of this existential suffering.

By practicing mindfulness with regard to feelings, you will gain an understanding of the truth of the origin of suffering. The insight achieved by this practice will make it clear that desire stems from pleasant feelings, leading to attachment and subsequent actions. Conversely, unpleasant feelings give rise to aversion; while neutral feelings, devoid of pleasure or discomfort, are accompanied by dullness. From desire, aversion, and dullness, various mental defilements emerge. Dullness, the lack of clear and conscious awareness, essentially forms the foundation for desire and aversion. You will also come to understand that the experience of feelings does not amount to a self. Practicing mindfulness with regard to feelings will lead to you becoming more aware of your feelings and thereby clearly recognizing the origin of suffering which is the second of the Noble Truths.

By practicing mindfulness with regard to the mind, you will gain an understanding of the third Noble Truth, the truth of the cessation of suffering. In this practice of directly observing the current states of the mind, you will experience their nature as fleeting and changing from moment to moment; this amounts to an immediate and direct cognition. Based on this direct cognition, you will become capable of drawing correct conclusions. Through this cognition based on inference, you will understand that the ultimate nature of these mental states goes beyond general cognitive processes and perceptions.

Thus, on the basis of your immediate experience, you will conceptually understand through cognition based on inference, that it is possible to actually experience the ultimate nature of the mind, that is, the deep and expansive "space of phenomena," emptiness. You will therefore confidently conclude that you will be able to put an end to suffering. Therefore, the application of mindfulness with regard to the mind will lead to an understanding of the cessation of suffering, the third Noble Truth.

By practicing mindfulness with regard to mental phenomena, the truth of the path reveals itself. This facet of the practice highlights the nature of mental defilements, showing everything that needs to be relinquished, along with the corresponding antidotes. Based on this insight, you will be able to proceed on the path, gaining access to the fourth Noble Truth.

Attaining freedom from suffering

Engaging in the consistent practice of the fourfold application of mindfulness paves the way for the liberation from existential disease, releasing you from the cycle of painful rebirth in the three realms of existence. As you overcome mental defilements, the fundamental causes of suffering, you will be able to attain complete freedom from suffering.

Most people worldwide do not grasp the true nature of the five aggregates, the skandhas. They fail to see them as they are—mere conditioned accumulations. Consequently, they undergo suffering. As an antidote to this suffering, the Buddha recommended the fourfold application of mindfulness, commencing with mindfulness with regard to the body and continuing with practicing mindfulness with regard to feelings, the mind, and mental phenomena. Thereby he illustrated how you will be able to transcend your clinging to distorted experiences and which remedies you should apply for this process, leading to freedom from suffering.

Text of the Tibetan Commentary (excerpt), the Basis for Shamar Rinpoche's Explanations

དོན་རྣམ་པར་གདོན་མི་ཟ་བའི་འགྲེལ་པ།[33]

... དགེ་སློང་དག་དྲན་པ་ཉེ་བར་གཞག་པ་བཞི་གང་ཞེ་ན་ཞེས་བྱ་བ་ནི་དྲིས་པའོ། །འདི་ལ་ཞེས་བྱ་བ་ནི། འདོད་པའི་ཁམས་འདིར་ཞེས་བྱ་བའི་དོན་ཏོ། །དགེ་སློང་ཞེས་བྱ་བ་ནི་དྲན་པ་ཉེ་བར་གཞག་པ་བཞི་བསྒོམ་པའི་རྣལ་འབྱོར་པའི་དགེ་སློང་ངོ་། །དེ་ཡང་ལུས་དྲན་པ་ཉེ་བར་གཞག་པ་དང་པོར་བཤད་དེ། དེ་ལ་ལུས་ནི་གང་། ལུས་ལ་ལུས་ཀྱི་རྗེས་སུ་ལྟ་བ་ནི་ཅི་ཞིག། །དྲན་པ་ནི་གང་། དྲན་པ་ཉེ་བར་

33 *Arthaviniścayasūtraṭīka.* Tibetan: *Don rnam par gdon mi za ba'i 'grel pa (The Commentary on the Discourse of Defining the Topics)*. Tibetan version in Tengyur D 4365, vol. 208, *sna tshogs* vol. *nyo*, 1b-192a. Excerpt: 140a1-147a1. Author and/or translator are unknown. It is a commentary on the sūtra: *Arthaviniścaya Nāma Dharmaparyāya.* Tibetan: *Don rnam par nges pa zhes bya ba'i chos kyi rnam grangs (The Dharma Discourse on Defining the Topics)*. Tibetan version in Kangyur H 321, vol. 72, *la* 262b-289a.

གཞག་པའི་དོན་ཡང་ཅི་ཞིག་ཅེ་ན། ལུས་གང་ཡིན་པ་ཇི་སྙ་བར་བྱའོ།

།དེ་ལ་ལུས་ནི་སུམ་ཅུ་རྩ་ལྔ་སྟེ། གང་ཞེ་ན། ནང་གི་དང་། ཕྱིའི་དང་། དབང་པོས་ཡོངས་སུ་བཟུང་བ་དང་། དབང་པོས་ཡོངས་སུ་མ་བཟུང་བ་དང་། སེམས་ཅན་གྱི་གྲངས་སུ་གཏོགས་པ་དང་། སེམས་ཅན་གྱི་གྲངས་སུ་མ་གཏོགས་པ་དང་། གནས་ངན་ལེན་པ་དང་བཅས་པ་དང་། བག་ཡངས་དང་བཅས་པ་དང་། འབྱུང་བའི་ལུས་དང་། འབྱུང་བ་ལས་གྱུར་པའི་ལུས་དང་། མིང་གི་ལུས་དང་། གཟུགས་ཀྱི་ལུས་དང་། དམྱལ་བའི་ལུས་དང་། བྱོལ་སོང་གི་དང་། ཡིད་དགས་ཀྱི་དང་། མིའི་དང་། ལྷ་དང་། རྣམ་པར་ཤེས་པ་དང་བཅས་པ་དང་རྣམ་པར་ཤེས་པ་མེད་པ་དང་། ནང་གི་ལུས་དང་། ཕྱིའི་ལུས་དང་། རྣམ་པར་གྱུར་པ་དང་། རྣམ་པར་མ་གྱུར་པ་དང་། བུད་མེད་ཀྱི་ལུས་དང་། སྐྱེས་པའི་ལུས་དང་། མ་ནིང་གི་ལུས་དང་། གྲོགས་ཀྱི་ལུས་དང་། གྲོགས་མ་ཡིན་པའི་ལུས་དང་། ཐ་མལ་བའི་ལུས་དང་། ལུས་ངན་པ་དང་། ལུས་འབྲིང་དང་། ལུས་དམ་པ་དང་། གྲོགས་པོའི་ལུས་དང་། ལང་ཚོའི་ལུས་དང་། རྒས་པའི་ལུས་ཏེ། འདི་དག་ནི་ཐང་ཅིག་ལུས་ཀྱི་རབ་ཏུ་དབྱེ་བའོ། །དེ་ལ་ནང་གི་ནི་བདག་ཉིད་ཀྱི་ལུས་སོ། །ཕྱིའི་ནི་གཞན་གྱི་ལུས་སོ། །དབང་པོས་ཡོངས་སུ་བཟུང་བ་ནི་མིག་ལ་སོགས་པའི་དབང་པོ་དང་བཅས་པའི་ལུས་སོ། །དབང་པོས་ཡོངས་སུ་མ་བཟུང་བ་ནི། གང་མིག་ལ་སོགས་པ་དབང་པོ་མེད་པ་སྟེ། ཀ་བ་དང་རྩིགས་ལ་སོགས་པའོ། །སེམས་ཅན་གྱི་གྲངས་སུ་གཏོགས་པ་ནི། གང་སེམས་དང་སེམས་ལས་བྱུང་བས་ཡོངས་སུ་བཟུང་བའོ། །སེམས་ཅན་གྱི་གྲངས་སུ་མ་གཏོགས་པ་ནི། གང་སེམས་དང་སེམས་ལས་བྱུང་ལས་བྱུང་བས་ཡོངས་སུ་མ་ཟིན་པའོ། །གནས་ངན་

ལེན་པ་དང་བཅས་པ་ནི། གང་ཉོན་མོངས་པ་མ་སྤྱངས་པའི་སེམས་ཅན་རྣམས་ཀྱིའོ། །བག་ཡངས་དང་བཅས་པ་ནི། གང་ཉོན་མོངས་པ་སྤྱོངས་པ་འཕགས་པ་རྣམས་ཀྱིའོ། །འབྱུང་བའི་ལུས་ནི་གང་ས་དང་། ཆུ་དང་། མེ་དང་། རླུང་རྣམས་སོ། །འབྱུང་བ་ལས་གྱུར་པའི་ལུས་ནི་གང་དབང་པོ་ལྔ་དང་ཡུལ་ལྔ་སྟེ་བཅུའོ། །མིང་གི་ལུས་ནི་རྣམ་པར་རིག་བྱེད་མ་ཡིན་པའི་གཟུགས་སམ། ཚོར་བ་དང་། འདུ་ཤེས་དང་། འདུ་བྱེད་དང་། རྣམ་པར་ཤེས་པའི་གཟུགས་རྣམས་སོ། །གཟུགས་ཀྱི་ལུས་ནི་གང་གཟུགས་ཀྱི་ཕུང་པོ་ཉིད་དོ། །དམྱལ་བའི་ལུས་ནི་གང་སེམས་ཅན་དམྱལ་བ་པ་རྣམས་ཀྱི་གཟུགས་སོ། །བྱོལ་སོང་གི་ལུས་ནི་གང་རྟ་དང་བ་ལང་ལ་སོགས་པའིའོ། །ཡི་དགས་ཀྱི་ལུས་ནི་གང་ཡི་དགས་རྣམས་ཀྱི་གཟུགས་སོ། །མིའི་ནི་གང་གླིང་བཞི་ན་གནས་པའི་མི་རྣམས་ཀྱི་གཟུགས་སོ། །ལྷའི་ནི་གང་འདོད་པ་དང་གཟུགས་དང་གཟུགས་མེད་པའི་ལྷ་རྣམས་ཀྱི་གཟུགས་སོ། །རྣམ་པར་ཤེས་པ་དང་བཅས་པ་ནི། གང་མིག་ལ་སོགས་པའི་རྣམ་པར་ཤེས་པ་དང་ལྡན་པའི་གཟུགས་དག་གོ། །རྣམ་པར་ཤེས་པ་མེད་པ་ནི་གང་མིག་ལ་སོགས་པའི་རྣམ་པར་ཤེས་པ་དང་མི་ལྡན་པ་སྟེ། འདུ་ཤེས་མེད་པ་དང་འགོག་པའི་སྙོམས་པར་འཇུག་པ་ལ་སོགས་པའི་གཟུགས་སོ། །ནང་གི་ནི་གང་ཤ་དང་ཁྲག་ལ་སོགས་པས་ཟིན་པའི་གཟུགས་སོ། །ཕྱིའི་ནི་གང་ཤ་དང་ཁྲག་ལ་སོགས་པས་ཡོངས་སུ་མ་ཟིན་པའི་གཟུགས་སོ། །རྣམ་པར་གྱུར་པ་ནི་གང་ཤི་ནས་བསྔོས་པ་དང་། བམ་པར་གྱུར་པའི་གཟུགས་སོ། །རྣམ་པར་མ་གྱུར་བ་ནི་གང་མ་ཤི་ལ་བསྔོས་པ་དང་བམ་པར་མ་གྱུར་བའི་གཟུགས་སོ། །བུད་མེད་ཀྱི་ལུས་ནི་གང་བུད་མེད་ཀྱི་དབང་པོ་དང་ལྡན་པའི་གཟུགས་སོ།

།སྐྱེས་པའི་ལུས་ནི་གང་སྐྱེས་པའི་དབང་པོ་དང་ལྡན་པའི་གཟུགས་སོ། །མ་ནིང་གི་ལུས་ནི་གང་མ་ནིང་གི་ལུས་མཚན་མ་ལྡན་པའི་གཟུགས་སོ། །གྲོགས་ཀྱི་ལུས་ནི་གང་བདག་དང་མཛའ་ཞིང་བཤེས་པར་གྱུར་པའི་སྐྱེ་བོ་རྣམས་ཀྱི་གཟུགས་སོ། །དེ་ལས་བཟློག་ན་གྲོགས་མ་ཡིན་པའི་ལུས་ཏེ། དགྲ་རྣམས་ཀྱི་གཟུགས་སོ། །ཐ་མལ་པའི་ལུས་ནི། གང་བདག་དང་བཤེས་པ་ཡང་མ་ཡིན་དགྲ་ཡང་མ་ཡིན་པའི་སྐྱེ་བོ་རྣམས་ཀྱི་གཟུགས་སོ། །ལུས་ངན་པ་ནི་གང་ཁ་དོག་དང་དབྱིབས་མི་མཛེས་པའི་གཟུགས་སོ། །ལུས་བར་མ་ནི་གང་ཁ་དོག་དང་དབྱིབས་མཛེས་པ་ཡང་མ་ཡིན། མི་མཛེས་པ་ཡང་མ་ཡིན་པའི་གཟུགས་སོ། །ལུས་དམ་པ་ནི་གང་ཁ་དོག་དང་དབྱིབས་མཛེས་པའོ། །གྲོགས་པོའི་ལུས་ནི་གང་བྱིས་པའི་དུས་ཀྱི་ལུས་སོ། །ཡང་ཆེའི་ལུས་ནི་དར་ལ་བབས་པའི་གཟུགས་སོ། །རྒས་པའི་གཟུགས་ནི་གང་དབང་པོ་དང་འབྱུང་བ་ཆེན་པོ་རྣམས་ལུས་ཞུམ་ཞིང་རྙིངས་པར་གྱུར་པའི་ལུས་སོ། །ལུས་དེ་དག་ཀྱང་བསྡུས་པ་ན་རྣམ་པ་གསུམ་དུ་འགྱུར་ཏེ། ནང་གི་ལུས་དང་ཕྱིའི་ལུས་དང་ཕྱི་ནང་གཉིས་ཀའི་ལུས་སོ། དེ་ལ་ནང་གི་ལུས་ནི་བདག་རང་ཉིད་ཀྱི་ལུས་ཏེ། སེམས་ཅན་གྱི་གྲངས་སུ་གཏོགས་པའོ། །ཕྱིའི་ལུས་ནི་གཟུགས་ལ་སོགས་པ་སྟེ། སེམས་ཅན་གྱི་གྲངས་སུ་མ་གཏོགས་པའོ། །ཕྱི་ནང་གཉིས་ཀའི་ལུས་ནི་སེམས་ཅན་གཞན་དག་གི་ལུས་སེམས་ཅན་གྱི་གྲངས་སུ་གཏོགས་པ་སྟེ། བདག་ལ་ལྟོས་ནས་གཞན་དུ་གྱུར་པས་ཕྱི་ཞེས་བྱའོ། །སེམས་ཅན་གྱི་གྲངས་སུ་གཏོགས་པས་ན་ནང་ཞེས་བྱའོ། །ཡང་ན་དབང་པོས་ཡོངས་སུ་ཟིན་པའི་གཟུགས་ནི་ནང་གི་ལུས་སོ། །དབང་པོས་ཡོངས་སུ་མ་ཟིན་པའི་གཟུགས་ནི་ཕྱིའི་ལུས་སོ། །གཞན་དག

གི་རྒྱུད་དུ་གཏོགས་པར་དབང་པོས་ཡོངས་སུ་ཟིན་པའི་གཟུགས་ནི་ཕྱི་ནང་གཉིས་ཀྱི་ལུས་སོ། །ཡང་ན་གང་མཉམ་པར་གཞག་པའི་ས་པ་བག་ཡངས་དང་བཅས་པའི་གཟུགས་ནི་ནང་གི་ལུས་སོ། །གང་བདག་ཉིད་ཀྱི་ལུས་མཉམ་པར་མ་གཞག་པའི་ས་པ་གནས་ངན་ལེན་དང་བཅས་པ་ནི་ཕྱིའི་ལུས་སོ། །གཞན་གྱི་ལུས་གནས་ངན་ལེན་དང་བཅས་པའམ། བག་ཡངས་དང་བཅས་པའི་གཟུགས་ནི་ཕྱི་ནང་གཉི་གའི་ལུས་སོ། །ཡང་ན་རྣམ་པར་ཤེས་པ་དང་བཅས་པའི་ལུས་ནི་ནང་གི་ལུས་སོ། །རྣམ་པར་ཤེས་པ་མེད་པའི་གཟུགས་སེམས་ཅན་གྱི་གྲངས་སུ་གཏོགས་པ་རྣམ་པར་བསྔོས་པ་དང་། རྣམ་པར་བམ་པ་ལ་སོགས་པའི་དུས་ན་ནི་ཕྱིའི་ལུས་སོ། །རྣམ་པར་ཤེས་པ་མེད་པའི་གཟུགས་སོ། །འདས་པའི་དུས་ན་རྣམ་པར་ཤེས་པ་དང་། བཅས་པ་དང་། རྣམ་པར་ཤེས་པ་དང་བཅས་པའི་གཟུགས་ཀྱང་མ་འོངས་པའི་དུས་ན། རྣམ་པར་ཤེས་པ་མེད་པར་འགྱུར་བ་ནི་ནང་དང་ཕྱིའི་ལུས་སོ། །ཡང་ན་སྐྲ་དང་སྤུ་དང་སེན་མོ་དང་ཁྲག་ལ་སོགས་པ་དང་ལྡན་པ་ནི་ནང་གི་ལུས་སོ། །གཞན་གྱི་སྐྲ་དང་སྤུ་དང་སེན་མོ་དང་ཁྲག་ལ་སོགས་པ་དང་བཅས་པ་ནི་ཕྱིའི་ལུས་སོ། །བདག་ཉིད་ཀྱི་ལུས་རྣམ་པར་བམ་པ་དང་། རྣམ་པར་བསྔོས་པ་ལ་སོགས་པའི་དུས་ན་ནི་ཕྱིའི་ལུས་ཏེ། འདི་ནི་ལུས་ཀྱི་རབ་ཏུ་དབྱེ་བའི་དོན་བསྡུས་པའོ།

།དེ་ལ་ལུས་ལ་ལུས་ཀྱི་རྗེས་སུ་ལྟ་བ་ཇི་ལྟ་བུ་ཞེ་ན། དེ་ནི་ཤེས་རབ་རྣམ་པ་གསུམ་སྟེ། མཉན་པ་ལས་བྱུང་བའི་ཤེས་རབ་དང་། བསམས་པ་ལས་བྱུང་བའི་ཤེས་རབ་དང་། བསྒོམས་པ་ལས་བྱུང་བའི་ཤེས་རབ་སྟེ། ཤེས་རབ་གང་གི་ལུས་ཀྱི་རང་བཞིན་རྣམ་པ་ཐམས་ཅད་དུ་ཁོང་དུ་ཆུད་ཅིང་རྟོགས་པར་བྱེད་པའོ།

།དེ་ལ་དྲན་པ་གང་ཞེ་ན། གང་གི་ལུས་ཀྱི་དབང་དུ་བྱས་ནས་བསྟན་པའི་ཆོས་དེ་དག་ཉེ་བར་བཟུང་ཞིང་ཆོས་གང་ཉེ་བར་བཟུང་བའི་དོན་རྣམས་སེམས་ཀྱི་བསམ་པ་དང་། བསྒོམས་པས་མངོན་སུམ་དུ་བྱས་པའི་ཡི་གེ་དང་དོན་རྣམས་ལ་མ་བརྗེད་པའོ།

།དྲན་པ་ཉེ་བར་གཞག་པའི་དོན་ཅི་ཞེ་ན། དེ་ཡང་རྣམ་པ་གསུམ་སྟེ། དྲན་པ་སྲུང་བར་བྱེད་པ་དང་། ཡུལ་ལ་ཀུན་ནས་ཉོན་མོངས་པ་མེད་པར་བྱེད་པ་དང་། དམིགས་པ་ལ་སེམས་ཉེ་བར་འཇོག་པར་བྱེད་པའོ། །དེ་ལ་དྲན་པ་སྲུང་བར་བྱེད་པ་ནི་དང་པོ་ནས་དབང་པོ་དང་། སེམས་རྣམས་ཡུལ་ལ་མི་འཇུག་པར་སྡོམ་པ་དང་། ཡུལ་ལ་ཀུན་ནས་ཉོན་མོངས་པ་མེད་པར་བྱེད་པ་ནི་ཡུལ་ལ་ཞུགས་ནས་ཡང་། གཟུགས་ལ་སོགས་པ་མཚན་མར་མི་འཛིན་བཟང་པོར་མི་འཛིན་པའོ། །དམིགས་པ་ལ་སེམས་ཉེ་བར་འཇོག་པར་བྱེད་པ་ནི། སྒོམ་པར་བྱེད་པའི་ཡུལ་ལ་སེམས་རྩེ་གཅིག་ཏུ་འཇོག་པའོ། །ནང་གི་ལུས་ལ་ལུས་ཀྱི་རྗེས་སུ་ལྟ་ཞིང་ཞེས་བྱ་བ་ལ་ནམ་བདག་ཉིད་ཀྱི་ལུས་སེམས་ཅན་གྱི་གྲངས་སུ་གཏོགས་པའི་གཟུགས་ལ་རང་དང་སྤྱིའི་མཚན་ཉིད་དུ་ཤེས་རབ་ཀྱིས་མཐོང་བར་བྱེད་པ་ནི། ནང་གི་ལུས་ལ་ལུས་ཀྱི་རྗེས་སུ་ལྟ་བ་ཞེས་བྱ་བ་སྟེ། ལུས་ཀྱི་རང་གི་མཚན་ཉིད་ནི། རྡུལ་ཕྲ་མོ་དུ་མ་བསགས་པ་ལས་གྲུར་པ་སྣབས་དང་། མཆིལ་མ་དང་། ཁྲག་དང་།ཆུ་སེར་ལ་སོགས་པ་མི་གཙང་བ་རྣམ་པ་སྣ་ཚོགས་ཀྱིས་གང་བའོ། །དེ་ལྟར་བསྒོམ་པ་ན་ཡང་གཉེན་པོས་གསལ་བར་མཐོང་བར་བྱ་བ་དང་། མི་མཐུན་པའི་ཕྱོགས་སྤངས་ནས་གནས་པར་བྱ་བ་སྟེ། རྣམ་པ་གཉིས་སོ། །དེ་ལ་གཉེན་པོ་ཡང་ཤེས་རབ་ཀྱིས་ལུས་ཀྱི་རང་གི་མཚན་ཉིད་མཐོང་བ་དང་། ཤེས་རབ་ཀྱིས་ལུས་ཀྱི་

སྤྱིའི་མཚན་ཉིད་མཐོང་བ་དང་། དེ་ལྟར་ཤེས་རབ་ཀྱིས་མཐོང་བའི་ཆོས་དེ་ལ་ཞི་གནས་རྩེ་གཅིག་ཏུ་འཇོག་པའོ། །མི་མཐུན་པའི་ཕྱོགས་ཀྱང་གཉིས་ཏེ། ལུས་དང་གཟུགས་ལ་སོགས་པའི་ཡུལ་ལ་ཆགས་པ་དང་། དེ་དག་ཉིད་ལ་ཁོང་ཁྲོ་བའི་ལུས་ཀྱི་རང་གི་མཚན་ཉིད་ཤེས་རབ་ཀྱིས་མི་གཙང་བ་ལ་སོགས་པར་ཕྱིན་ཅི་མ་ལོག་པར་མཐོང་བ་ནི་གསལ་བའོ། །ལུས་ཀྱི་སྤྱིའི་མཚན་ཉིད་ཤེས་རབ་ཀྱིས་ཕྱིན་ཅི་མ་ལོག་པར་མཐོང་བ་ནི་ཡང་དག་པར་རབ་ཏུ་ཤེས་པའོ། །ཤེས་རབ་ཀྱིས་ལུས་ཀྱི་རང་དང་སྤྱིའི་མཚན་ཉིད་མཐོང་བ་དེ་ཉིད་ཀྱི་དོན་མ་བརྗེད་ཅིང་དེ་ལ་རྟག་ཏུ་ཞི་གནས་ཀྱི་སེམས་རྩེ་གཅིག་ཏུ་འཇོག་པ་ནི་དྲན་པ་དང་ལྡན་པའི། །ལུས་དྲན་པ་ཉེ་བར་གཞག་པའི་བར་དུ་གཅོད་པའི་མི་མཐུན་པའི་ཕྱོགས་སུ་གྱུར་པ་ལུས་དང་གཟུགས་ལ་སོགས་པ་ལ་ཆགས་པ་སྤངས་པ་ནི་འཇིག་རྟེན་གྱི་ཆགས་པ་དང་བྲལ་བའོ། །དེའི་བར་དུ་གཅོད་པ་ཞེ་སྡང་སྤངས་པ་ནི། ཡིད་མི་བདེ་བ་སྤངས་པ་ཞེས་བྱའོ། །གནས་པའི་གོང་དུ་བཤད་པ་ལྟར་བསྒོམ་པའོ། །ནམ་ཕྱིའི་ལུས་གཟུགས་ལ་སོགས་པ་སེམས་ཅན་གྱི་གྲངས་སུ་མ་གཏོགས་པ་རྣམས་ཀྱིས་རང་དང་སྤྱིའི་མཚན་ཉིད་རྟོགས་པར་བྱེད་པ་ནི། ཕྱིའི་ལུས་ལ་ལུས་ཀྱི་རྗེས་སུ་ལྟ་ཞིང་གནས་པ་ཞེས་བྱ་སྟེ། རང་གི་མཚན་ཉིད་ནི་རྡུལ་ཕྲ་རབ་བསགས་པའི་ངོ་བོའོ། །ཕྱིའི་མཚན་ཉིད་ནི་མི་རྟག་པ་དང་། སྡུག་བསྔལ་བ་དང་། སྟོང་པ་དང་བདག་མེད་པ་སྟེ། གསལ་བ་ཡང་དག་པར་རབ་ཏུ་ཤེས་པ་ཡང་དེའི་སྐད་དུ་སྦྱར་ཞིང་། དེ་དག་གི་དོན་ཡང་སྔར་བསྟན་པ་བཞིན་དུ་བལྟའོ། །སེམས་ཅན་གཞན་དག་གི་ལས་སེམས་ཅན་གྱི་གྲངས་སུ་གཏོགས་པའི་རང་དང་སྤྱིའི་མཚན་ཉིད་རྟོགས་པར་བྱེད་པ་ནི། ནང་དང་ཕྱིའི་ལུས་ལ་ལུས་ཀྱི་རྗེས་སུ་ལྟ་

བ་ཞེས་བྱ་སྟེ། རང་དང་སྤྱིའི་མཚན་ཉིད་ཀྱང་གོང་དུ་བཤད་པ་བཞིན་དུ་བལྟའོ།

།ནང་གི་ཚོར་བ་དང་ཕྱིའི་ཚོར་བ་དང་ཞེས་བྱ་བ་ལ་སོགས་པ་དེ་ལ་ཚོར་བ་གང་ཞེ་ན། འདི་ལྟ་སྟེ་བདེ་བ་དང་། སྡུག་བསྔལ་བ་དང་། བདེ་བ་ཡང་མ་ཡིན་སྡུག་བསྔལ་བ་ཡང་མ་ཡིན་པའི་ཚོར་བའོ། །བདེ་བ་དང་སྡུག་བསྔལ་བ་དང་། བདེ་བ་ཡང་མ་ཡིན་སྡུག་བསྔལ་བ་ཡང་མ་ཡིན་པའི་ཚོར་བ་ལ་ཡང་ལུས་དང་ལྡན་པ་དང་། དེ་བཞིན་དུ་སེམས་དང་ལྡན་པའོ། །ཚོར་བ་ལ་སོགས་པ་བདེ་བ་ཡང་ཟང་ཟིང་དང་བཅས་པ་དང་། ཟང་ཟིང་མེད་པ་དང་། ཆགས་པ་ལ་བརྟེན་པ་དང་། འབྱུང་བ་ལ་བརྟེན་པ་སྟེ། འདི་དག་ནི་ཚོར་བའི་རབ་ཏུ་དབྱེ་བའོ། །དེ་ལ་ལུས་དང་སེམས་ལ་སིམ་པ་ཕན་པར་བྱེད་པ་ནི་བདེ་བའི་ཚོར་བའོ། །ལུས་དང་སེམས་ལ་གནོད་པ་ལས་གདུང་བར་བྱེད་པ་ནི་སྡུག་བསྔལ་གྱི་ཚོར་བའོ། །ལུས་དང་སེམས་ལ་ཕན་པར་ཡང་མི་བྱེད། གདུང་བར་ཡང་མི་བྱེད་པ་ནི། བདེ་བ་ཡང་མ་ཡིན། སྡུག་བསྔལ་བ་ཡང་མ་ཡིན་པའི་ཚོར་བའོ། །ཚོར་བ་དེ་གསུམ་ཡང་ནམ་མིག་གི་རྣམ་པར་ཤེས་པ་ནས་ལུས་ཀྱི་རྣམ་པར་ཤེས་པ་ལྔ་དང་འབྲེལ་བའི་དུས་ན་ནི་ལུས་དང་ལྡན་པའོ། །ཚོར་བ་དེ་གསུམ་ཡིད་ཀྱི་རྣམ་པར་ཤེས་པ་དང་འབྲེལ་པའི་དུས་ན་ནི་སེམས་དང་ལྡན་པའོ། །ཚོར་བ་གསུམ་མྱ་ངན་ལས་འདས་པ་དང་རྗེས་སུ་མཐུན་པར་གྱུར་ན་ནི། ཟང་ཟིང་མེད་པའོ། །ཁམས་གསུམ་དུ་གཏོགས་པའི་ཚོར་བ་ཐམས་ཅད་ནི་ཟང་ཟིང་དང་བཅས་པའོ། །ནམ་འཕགས་པའི་ལམ་དང་རྗེས་སུ་མཐུན་པར་གྱུར་པ་ནི། འབྱུང་བ་ལ་བརྟེན་པའོ། །འདོད་པའི་ཡོན་ཏན་ལྔ་ལ་ཞེན་པ་ནི་ཞེན་པ་ལ་བརྟེན་པ་ཞེས་བྱའོ། །དེ་ལ་རྗེས་

སུ་ལྟ་བ་དང་དྲན་པ་དང་། དྲན་པ་ཉེ་བར་གཞག་པ་གང་ཡིན་པའི་དོན་རྣམས་ནི་ལུས་དྲན་པ་ཉེ་བར་གཞག་པའི་སྐབས་སུ་བཤད་པ་བཞིན་དུ་བལྟའོ། །དེ་ལ་བདག་ཉིད་ཀྱི་ལུས་སེམས་ཅན་གྱི་གྲངས་སུ་གཏོགས་པ་ལ་དམིགས་པ་ལས། ཚོར་བ་བདེ་བ་དང་། སྡུག་བསྔལ་དང་། བདེ་བ་ཡང་མ་ཡིན། སྡུག་བསྔལ་ཡང་མ་ཡིན་པ་སྐྱེས་པ་ནི་ནང་གི་ཚོར་བའོ། །གཟུགས་ལ་སོགས་པའི་སེམས་ཅན་གྱི་གྲངས་སུ་མ་གཏོགས་པ་ལས་ཚོར་བ་བདེ་བ་ལ་སོགས་པ་སྐྱེས་པ་ནི་ཕྱིའི་ཚོར་བའོ། །སེམས་ཅན་གཞན་དག་གི་ལུས་སེམས་ཅན་གྱི་གྲངས་སུ་གཏོགས་པ་ལ་དམིགས་པ་ལས། ཚོར་བ་བདེ་བ་ལ་སོགས་པ་སྐྱེས་པ་ནི་ནང་དང་ཕྱིའི་ཚོར་བ་ཞེས་བྱ་སྟེ། ཚོར་བ་རྣམ་པ་གསུམ་ཡང་སྡུག་བསྔལ་དང་འབྲེལ་པར་མཐོང་བ་ནི། ཚོར་བ་ལ་ཚོར་བའི་རྗེས་སུ་བལྟ་ཞིང་དྲན་པ་ཉེ་བར་གཞག་པའོ། །སྡུག་བསྔལ་གསུམ་ལ་སྡུག་བསྔལ་གྱི་སྡུག་བསྔལ་དང་། འགྱུར་བའི་སྡུག་བསྔལ་དང་། འདུ་བྱེད་ཀྱི་སྡུག་བསྔལ་བའོ། །དེ་ལ་སྡུག་བསྔལ་གྱི་ཚོར་བ་ནི་སྡུག་བསྔལ་གྱི་སྡུག་བསྔལ་དང་འབྲེལ། བདེ་བའི་ཚོར་བ་ནི་ཐང་ཅིག་བདེར་ཟིན་ཀྱང་ཕྱིས་སྡུག་བསྔལ་གྱི་རྒྱུར་འགྱུར་བས་ན་འགྱུར་བའི་སྡུག་བསྔལ་དང་འབྲེལ། བདེ་བ་ཡང་མ་ཡིན་སྡུག་བསྔལ་ཡང་མ་ཡིན་པའི་ཚོར་བ་ནི་མི་རྟག་པའི་ཆོས་དང་ལྡན་པས་ན་འདུ་བྱེད་ཀྱི་སྡུག་བསྔལ་དང་འབྲེལ་ཏེ། གསལ་བ་ལ་སོགས་པའི་དོན་ནི་གོང་དུ་བཤད་པ་བཞིན་དུ་བལྟའོ།

།ནང་གི་སེམས་དང་ཞེས་བྱ་བ་ལ་སོགས་པ་སེམས་དབྱེ་ན་རྣམ་པ་ཉི་ཤུ་སྟེ། འདོད་ཆགས་དང་བཅས་པའི་སེམས་དང་། འདོད་ཆགས་དང་བྲལ་བའི་སེམས་དང་། ཞེ་སྡང་དང་བཅས་པའི་སེམས་

དང་། ཞེ་སྡང་དང་བྲལ་བའི་སེམས་དང་། གཏི་མུག་དང་བཅས་པའི་སེམས་དང་། གཏི་མུག་དང་བྲལ་བའི་སེམས་དང་། འདུས་པའི་སེམས་དང་། རྣམ་པར་གཡེང་བའི་སེམས་དང་། ཞུམ་པའི་སེམས་དང་། གཟེངས་མཐོ་བའི་སེམས་དང་། རྒོད་པའི་སེམས་དང་། རྒོད་པ་མེད་པའི་སེམས་དང་། ཞི་བའི་སེམས་དང་། མ་ཞི་བའི་སེམས་དང་། ཤིན་ཏུ་མཉམ་པར་གཞག་པའི་སེམས་དང་། ཤིན་ཏུ་མཉམ་པར་གཞག་པ་མ་ཡིན་པའི་སེམས་དང་། ལམ་ཤིན་ཏུ་བསྒོམ་པའི་སེམས་དང་། ལམ་ཤིན་ཏུ་བསྒོམ་པ་མ་ཡིན་པའི་སེམས་དང་། ཤིན་ཏུ་བསྒོམ་པ་ལས་གྲོལ་བའི་སེམས་དང་། ཤིན་ཏུ་བསྒོམ་པ་ལས་གྲོལ་བ་མ་ཡིན་པའི་སེམས་སོ། །དེ་ལ་གང་ཆགས་པར་བྱ་བའི་དངོས་པོ་ལ་འདོད་ཆགས་ཀྱིས་ཀུན་ནས་དཀྲིས་པ་མངོན་སུམ་དུ་སྤྱོད་པ་ནི། འདོད་ཆགས་དང་བཅས་པའི་སེམས་ཞེས་བྱའོ། །འདོད་ཆགས་ཀྱིས་ཀུན་ནས་དཀྲིས་པ་བག་ལ་ཉལ་ཙམ་དུ་ཟད་ཀྱི། དངོས་སུ་སྤྱོད་པ་མེད་པ་ནི། འདོད་ཆགས་དང་བྲལ་བའི་སེམས་ཞེས་བྱའོ། །ཞེ་སྡང་གི་དངོས་པོ་ལ་ཞེ་སྡང་གི་ཀུན་ནས་དཀྲིས་པ་མངོན་སུམ་དུ་སྤྱོད་པ་ནི། ཞེ་སྡང་དང་བཅས་པའི་སེམས་ཞེས་བྱའོ། །ཞེ་སྡང་བག་ལ་ཉལ་ཙམ་དུ་ཟད་ཀྱི། དངོས་སུ་བྱུང་བ་མེད་པ་ནི། ཞེ་སྡང་དང་བྲལ་བའི་སེམས་ཞེས་བྱའོ། །ཀུན་ཏུ་གཏི་མུག་པར་གྱུར་པའི་དངོས་པོ་ལ་རྨོངས་པ་ཀུན་ཏུ་འབྱུང་བ་ནི། གཏི་མུག་དང་བཅས་པའི་སེམས་ཞེས་བྱའོ། །གཏི་མུག་བག་ལ་ཉལ་ཙམ་དུ་གནས་པ་ནི། །གཏི་མུག་དང་བྲལ་བའི་སེམས་ཞེས་བྱ་སྟེ། སེམས་དྲུག་པོ་དེ་དག་ནི་ཀུན་ཏུ་སྤྱོད་པའི་དུས་ན་འབྱུང་བ་ལས་གཞག་པར་རིག་པར་བྱའོ། །དེ་ལ་གསུམ་ནི་ཀུན་ནས་ཉོན་མོངས་པའི་ཕྱོགས་སོ། །གསུམ་ནི་དེ་དག

གི་གཉེན་པོའི་ཕྱོགས་སོ། །དེ་ལ་ཞི་གནས་ཀྱི་རྣམ་པར་སེམས་ནང་
དུ་གནས་པར་གྱུར་པ་འདུས་པའི་སེམས་སོ། །འདོད་པའི་ཡོན་ཏན་
ལྔའི་རྗེས་སུ་འབྲང་བ་གཡེངས་པའི་སེམས་སོ། །གཉིད་དང་རྨུགས་
པ་དང་ལྡན་པ་ནི་ཞུམ་པའི་སེམས་སོ། གཉིད་དང་རྨུགས་པ་སེལ་
བར་བྱེད་པའི་ཆོས་རབ་ཏུ་དང་བར་བྱེད་པ་འགའ་ཞིག་ལ་དམིགས་
ནས་སེམས་དགའ་བར་བྱས་པ་ནི་གཟེངས་མཐོས་པའི་སེམས་སོ།
།སེམས་གཟེངས་བསྟོད་པ་ལས་སླར་གཡེངས་བར་གྱུར་པ་ནི་རྒོད་
པའི་སེམས་སོ། །ཞུམ་རྒོད་སྤངས་ནས་སེམས་བཏང་སྙོམས་སུ་གྱུར་
པ་ནི་རྒོད་པ་མེད་པའི་སེམས་སོ། །གཉིད་དང་རྨུགས་པ་དང་འགྱོད་
པ་དང་ཐེ་ཚོམ་ལ་སོགས་པའི་སྒྲིབ་པ་དང་བྲལ་བ་ནི་ཞི་བའི་སེམས་
སོ། །སྒྲིབ་པ་དེ་དག་དང་མ་བྲལ་བ་ནི་མ་ཞི་བའི་སེམས་སོ། །རྩ་
བའི་བསམ་གཏན་བཞི་ལ་ཞུགས་པ་ནི་ཤིན་ཏུ་མཉམ་པར་གཞག་
པའི་སེམས་སོ། །རྩ་བའི་བསམ་གཏན་བཞི་ལ་མ་ཞུགས་པ་ནི་ཤིན་
ཏུ་མཉམ་པར་མ་གཞག་པའི་སེམས་སོ། །རྩ་བའི་བསམ་གཏན་དེ་
དག་ཉིད་ལ་ཤིན་ཏུ་བསྒོམས་པ་དང་། དུས་རིང་དུ་བསྒོམས་པས་ཅི་
དགར་དབང་དུ་གྱུར་པ་ནི་ལམ་ཤིན་ཏུ་བསྒོམ་པའི་སེམས་སོ། །རྩ་
བའི་བསམ་གཏན་ཐོབ་ཀྱང་ཤིན་ཏུ་མ་བསྒོམས་ལ། དུས་རིང་དུ་མ་
བསྒོམས་པས་ཅི་དགར་དབང་ཐོབ་པར་མ་གྱུར་པ་ནི། ལམ་ཤིན་ཏུ་
བསྒོམ་པ་མ་ཡིན་པའི་སེམས་སོ། །ལམ་ཤིན་ཏུ་བསྒོམས་པ་ལས་
ཉོན་མོངས་པ་ཐམས་ཅད་བྱུང་བ་དང་། ཤིན་ཏུ་བྱུང་བ་ནི་ཤིན་ཏུ་
བསྒོམས་པས་གྲོལ་བའི་སེམས་སོ། །ཉོན་མོངས་པ་ཐམས་ཅད་དང་
ཤིན་ཏུ་བྱུང་བ་མ་ཡིན་པའི་ཉོན་མོངས་པ་ཁ་ཅིག་བྱུང་བ་ནི་ཤིན་ཏུ་
བསྒོམས་པས་གྲོལ་བ་མ་ཡིན་པའི་སེམས་ཏེ། སེམས་བཅུ་དྲུག་པོ་

དེ་དག་ནི་གནས་པའི་དུས་ཀྱི་དབང་དུ་བྱས་ནས་བཤད་པར་རིག་པར་བྱའོ། །སེམས་ཉི་ཤུ་པོ་དེ་དག་ཀྱང་མདོར་བསྡུ་ན་རྣམ་པ་གསུམ་སྟེ། ནང་གི་སེམས་དང་། ཕྱིའི་སེམས་དང་། ཕྱི་ནང་གི་སེམས་སོ། །དེ་ལ་བདག་གི་ལུས་སེམས་ཅན་གྱི་གྲངས་སུ་གཏོགས་པ་ལས་དམིགས་པ་ལས་སེམས་ཉི་ཤུ་པོ་བྱུང་བ་ནི་ནང་གི་སེམས་ཞེས་བྱའོ། །གཟུགས་ལ་སོགས་པ་སེམས་ཅན་གྱི་གྲངས་སུ་མ་གཏོགས་པ་ལ་དམིགས་པ་ལས་སེམས་ཉི་ཤུ་པོ་དེ་དག་བྱུང་བ་ནི་ཕྱིའི་སེམས་ཞེས་བའོ། །སེམས་ཅན་གཞན་གྱི་གཟུགས་སེམས་ཅན་གཞན་གྱི་གྲངས་སུ་གཏོགས་པ་ལ་སེམས་དམིགས་པ་ལས་སེམས་ཉི་ཤུ་པོ་དེ་དག་བྱུང་བ་ནི་ནང་དང་ཕྱིའི་སེམས་ཞེས་བྱ་སྟེ། སེམས་ལ་ཡང་སྐད་ཅིག་ཏུ་འདོད་ཆགས་དང་བཅས་པ་དང་། སྐད་ཅིག་ཏུ་འདོད་ཆགས་དང་བྲལ་བ་ལ་སོགས་པར་འགྱུར་ཏེ། སྐད་ཅིག་ཀྱང་མི་གནས་པ་རང་བཞིན་གཞན་དང་དུ་འགྱུར་བར་རྟོགས་པར་བྱེད་པ་ནི། སེམས་ལ་སེམས་ཀྱི་རྗེས་སུ་ལྟ་བ་ཞེས་བྱ་སྟེ། གསལ་བ་ལ་སོགས་པའི་དོན་གཞན་ནི་གོང་དུ་བཤད་པར་ཟད་དོ།

།ནང་གི་ཆོས་དང་ཞེས་བྱ་བ་ལ་སོགས་པ་ལ་ཆོས་ནི་ནག་པོའི་ཕྱོགས་དང་། དཀར་པོའི་ཕྱོགས་རྣམ་པ་གཉིས་ལས་དབྱེ་ན། རྣམ་པ་ཉི་ཤུར་རིག་པར་བྱའོ། །ཉི་ཤུ་པོ་དེ་དག་གང་ཞེ་ན། འདོད་ཆགས་དང་འདོད་ཆགས་འདུལ་བ་དང་། ཞེ་སྡང་དང་ཞེ་སྡང་འདུལ་བ་དང་། གཏི་མུག་དང་གཏི་མུག་འདུལ་བ་དང་། འདུས་པ་དང་། རྣམ་པར་གཡེངས་པ་དང་། ཞུམ་པ་དང་། གཟེངས་མཐོས་པ་དང་། རྒོད་པ་དང་། རྒོད་པ་མེད་པ་དང་། ཞི་བ་དང་། མ་ཞི་བ་དང་། ཤིན་ཏུ་མཉམ་པར་གཞག་པ་དང་། ཤིན་ཏུ་མཉམ་པར་གཞག་པ་མ་ཡིན་

པ་དང་། ལམ་ཤིན་ཏུ་བསྒོམས་པ་དང་། ལམ་ཤིན་ཏུ་བསྒོམས་པ་མ་ཡིན་པ་དང་། ཤིན་ཏུ་བསྒོམས་པས་གྲོལ་བ་དང་། ཤིན་ཏུ་བསྒོམས་པས་གྲོལ་བ་མ་ཡིན་པ་སྟེ། འདོད་ཆགས་དང་། ཞེ་སྡང་དང་། གཏི་མུག་དང་། གཡེངས་པ་དང་། ཞུམ་པ་དང་། རྒོད་པ་དང་། མ་ཞི་བ་དང་། མཉམ་པར་མ་བཞག་པ་དང་། ལམ་ལེགས་པར་མ་བསྒོམས་པ་དང་། ལེགས་པར་བསྒོམས་པས་གྲོལ་བ་མེད་པ་སྟེ། བཅུ་ནི་ནག་པོའི་ཕྱོགས་སོ། །འདོད་ཆགས་འདུལ་བ་དང་། ཞེ་སྡང་འདུལ་བ་དང་། གཏི་མུག་འདུལ་བ་དང་། འདུས་པ་དང་། གཟེངས་མཐོས་པ་དང་། མི་རྒོད་པ་དང་། ཞི་བ་དང་། མཉམ་པར་གཞག་པ་དང་། ལམ་ལེགས་པར་བསྒོམས་པ་དང་། ལེགས་པར་བསྒོམས་པས་གྲོལ་བ་སྟེ་བཅུ་ནི་དཀར་པོའི་ཕྱོགས་སོ། །དེ་ལ་གཟུགས་དང་འདོད་པའི་ཡོན་ཏན་ལ་ཆགས་པ་ནི་འདོད་ཆགས་སོ། །མི་གཙང་བ་བསྒོམ་པ་ནི་འདོད་ཆགས་འདུལ་བའོ། །དགྲ་ལ་སོགས་པ་ལ་ཁོང་ཁྲོ་བ་ནི་ཞེ་སྡང་ངོ་། །བྱམས་པ་ནི་ཞེ་སྡང་འདུལ་བའོ། །ལས་དང་ལས་ཀྱི་འབྲས་བུ་མི་ཤེས་པ་ནི་གཏི་མུག་གོ། །ཆོས་རྣམས་ཀྱི་རང་དང་སྤྱིའི་མཚན་ཉིད་ཤེས་པའི་ཤེས་རབ་ནི་གཏི་མུག་འདུལ་བའོ། །སེམས་ནང་དུ་རྩེ་གཅིག་ཏུ་གནས་པ་ནི་འདུས་པའོ། །སེམས་འདོད་པའི་ཡོན་ཏན་ལ་ཞུགས་པ་ནི་གཡེངས་པའོ། །སེམས་གཉིད་དང་རྨུགས་པས་ནོན་པ་ནི་ཞུམ་པའོ། །བསམ་གཏན་གྱི་འབྲས་བུའམ། དེ་བཞིན་གཤེགས་པའི་ཡོན་ཏན་བསམས་ནས་གཉིད་དང་རྨུགས་པ་བསལ་བ་ནི་གཟེངས་མཐོས་པའོ། །སེམས་གཟེངས་བསྟོད་པ་ལས་སླར་སེམས་འཕྲོས་པར་གྱུར་པ་ནི་རྒོད་པའོ། །ཞུམ་རྒོད་གཉིས་སྤངས་ཏེ་སེམས་མཉམ་པར་གྱུར་པ་ནི་རྒོད་པ་མེད་པའོ། །གཉིད་དང་རྨུགས་པ་ལ་

སོགས་པའི་སྒྲིབ་པ་དང་བྲལ་བ་ནི་ཞི་བའོ། །སྒྲིབ་པ་དང་མ་བྲལ་བ་ནི་ཞི་བའོ། །བསམ་གཏན་དང་པོ་དང་གཉིས་པ་དང་གསུམ་པ་དང་བཞི་པ་སྟེ། རྩ་བའི་བསམ་གཏན་ལ་ཞུགས་པ་ནི། ཤིན་ཏུ་མཉམ་པར་གཞག་པའོ། །རྩ་བའི་བསམ་གཏན་ལམ་ཞུགས་པ་ནི་མཉམ་པར་གཞག་པ་མ་ཡིན་པའོ། །དེ་ལ་འཕགས་པའི་ལམ་བསྒོམ་པ་ཐོབ་པ་ནི། ལམ་ཤིན་ཏུ་བསྒོམས་པའོ། །འཕགས་པའི་ལམ་བསྒོམ་པ་མ་ཐོབ་པ་ནི། ལམ་ཤིན་ཏུ་བསྒོམས་པ་མ་ཡིན་པའོ། །ཁམས་གསུམ་གྱི་ཉོན་མོངས་པ་ཐམས་ཅད་སྤངས་ནས་ཕྱིས་མི་སྐྱེ་བ་ནི་ཤིན་ཏུ་བསྒོམས་པས་གྲོལ་བའོ། །ཉོན་མོངས་པ་མ་ལུས་པར་སྤངས་པ་མ་ཡིན་པ་ནི་ཤིན་ཏུ་བསྒོམས་པས་གྲོལ་བ་མ་ཡིན་པའོ། །ཆོས་དེ་དག་ཀྱང་རྣམ་པ་གསུམ་དུ་བཞག་སྟེ། ནང་གི་ཆོས་དང་། ཕྱིའི་ཆོས་དང་། ནང་དང་ཕྱིའི་ཆོས་སོ། །དེ་ལ་བདག་རང་ཉིད་ཀྱི་ལུས་སེམས་ཅན་གྱི་གྲངས་སུ་གཏོགས་པ་ལས་ནག་པོ་འམ་དཀར་པོའི་ཆོས་བྱུང་བ་ནི་ནང་གི་ཆོས་སོ། །གཟུགས་ལ་སོགས་པ་སེམས་ཅན་གྱི་གྲངས་སུ་མ་གཏོགས་པ་ལ་དམིགས་པ་ལས། དཀར་པོའམ། ནག་པོའི་ཆོས་བྱུང་བ་ནི། ཕྱིའི་ཆོས་སོ། །སེམས་ཅན་གཞན་གྱི་ལུས་སེམས་ཅན་གྱི་གྲངས་སུ་གཏོགས་པ་ལ་དམིགས་པ་ལས་དཀར་པོའམ་ནག་པོའི་ཆོས་བྱུང་བ་ནི། ནང་དང་ཕྱིའི་ཆོས་ཞེས་བྱ་སྟེ། ནག་པོའི་ཆོས་ཀྱིས་ནི་ཀུན་ནས་ཉོན་མོངས་པར་འགྱུར། དཀར་པོའི་ཆོས་ཀྱིས་ནི་རྣམ་པར་བྱང་བར་འགྱུར་བ་ཙམ་དུ་ཟད་ཀྱི། འདི་ན་ཀུན་ནས་ཉོན་མོངས་པར་བྱེད་པའི་བདག་གམ། རྣམ་པར་བྱང་བར་བྱེད་པའི་བདག་མེད་དོ་ཞེས་ལྟ་བ་ནི་ཆོས་ལ་ཆོས་ཀྱི་རྗེས་སུ་ལྟ་བ་ཞེས་བྱ་བ་སྟེ། གསལ་བ་ལ་སོགས་པའི་དོན་ནི་གོང་དུ་བཤད་པ་བཞིན་ནོ།

།དེ་ལ་དྲན་པ་ཉེ་བར་གཞག་པ་བཞི་ཡང་རྣམ་པར་ལྔར་རྣམ་པར་གཞག་སྟེ། རྣམ་པ་ལྔ་ནི་དམིགས་པ་དང་། རང་བཞིན་དང་། གྲོགས་དང་། བསྒོམ་པ་དང་། བསྒོམས་པའི་འབྲས་བུའོ། །ཇི་ལྟར་ན་དྲན་པ་ཉེ་བར་གཞག་པ་བཞི་ལ་རྣམ་པ་ལྔར་རྣམ་པར་གཞག་པ་བཞིན་དུ། བྱང་ཆུབ་ཀྱི་ཕྱོགས་ལྷག་མ་རྣམས་ལ་ཡང་རྣམ་པ་ལྔ་ལྔར་གཞག་གོ།

།དྲན་པ་ཉེ་བར་གཞག་པའི་དམིགས་པ་གང་ཞེ་ན། དེ་ཡང་བཞི་སྟེ། ལུས་དང་། སེམས་དང་། ཚོར་བ་དང་། ཆོས་སོ། །ཡང་ན་བདག་གི་རྟེན་གྱི་དངོས་པོ་དང་། བདག་ཀུན་ནས་ལོངས་སྤྱོད་པའི་དངོས་པོ་དང་། བདག་ཉིད་ཀྱི་དངོས་པོ་དང་། བདག་ཀུན་ནས་ཉོན་མོངས་པ་དང་། རྣམ་པར་བྱང་བར་བྱེད་པའི་དངོས་པོ་སྟེ། དེ་བཞི་ནི་དྲན་པ་ཉེ་བར་གཞག་པའི་དམིགས་པར་བྱའོ། །དེ་ལ་བདག་གི་དངོས་པོ་ནི་ལུས་སོ། །བདག་ཀུན་ནས་ལོངས་སྤྱོད་པར་བྱེད་པའི་དངོས་པོ་ནི་ཚོར་བའོ། །བདག་ཉིད་ཀྱི་དངོས་པོ་ནི་སེམས་སོ། །བདག་ཀུན་ནས་ཉོན་མོངས་པ་དང་། རྣམ་པར་བྱང་བར་བྱེད་པའི་དངོས་པོ་ནི་ཆོས་སོ། །དེ་ལ་ཡང་ཇི་ལྟར་དམིགས་པ་ཞེ་ན། བློ་ཕྱིན་ཅི་ལོག་ཏུ་གྱུར་པའི་བྱིས་པ་དག་ཕལ་ཆེར་དབང་པོ་དང་བཅས་པའི་ལུས་ལ་བདག་བརྟེན་ཅིང་བདེ་བ་ལ་སོགས་པ་ཀུན་ཏུ་ལོངས་སྤྱོད་པར་བྱེད་ལ། དེ་ལྟར་ཀུན་ཏུ་ལོངས་སྤྱོད་པར་བྱེད་པའི་བདག་དེ་ཡང་སེམས་ཉིད་ཡིན་ཏེ། བདག་དེ་འདོད་ཆགས་ལ་སོགས་པས་ནི་ཀུན་ནས་ཉོན་མོངས་པར་འགྱུར་ལ། དད་པ་ལ་སོགས་པས་ནི་རྣམ་པར་བྱང་བར་འགྱུར་ཏེ། ཞེས་རྟོགས་པར་བྱ་བའི་ཕྱིར། ལུས་ལ་སོགས་པ་བསྒོམ་ཞིང་རྣམ་པར་གཞག་གོ།

།རང་བཞིན་གང་ཞེ་ན། ཤེས་རབ་དང་ཞི་གནས་ཏེ། ལུས་ལ་རྗེས་སུ་ལྟ་བ་ཞེས་སྨྲ་བས་ཤེས་རས་སྨྲ་བ་ཡིན། །དྲན་པ་དང་ལྡན་པ་དང་། གནས་པ་ཞེས་སྨྲས་པས་ཞི་གནས་བསྟན་པ་ཡིན་ནོ།

།གྲོགས་པོ་ནི་དེ་དང་ལྡན་པའི་སེམས་དང་སེམས་ལས་བྱུང་བ་རྣམས་ཏེ། ཤེས་རབ་དང་ཞི་གནས་གཉིས་ཀྱང་བརྩོན་འགྲུས་ལ་སོགས་པའི་སེམས་ལས་བྱུང་བ་གཞན་དང་མི་ལྡན་པ་འབའ་ཞིག་འབྱུང་མི་སྲིད་པའི་ཕྱིར་རོ།

།བསྒོམ་པ་ནི་ནང་དང་ཕྱི་དང་ཕྱི་ནང་གཉིས་ཀྱི་ལུས་ཀྱི་རང་དང་སྤྱིའི་མཚན་ཉིད་གོམས་པར་བྱའོ།

།བསྒོམས་པའི་འབྲས་བུ་ནི་ཕྱིན་ཅི་ལོག་བཞི་སྤངས་པ་དང་། བདེན་པ་ཞི་ལ་འཇུག་པ་དང་། ལུས་ལ་སོགས་པ་དང་བྲལ་བར་འགྱུར་བའོ། །དེ་ལ་ཕྱིན་ཅི་ལོག་བཞི་ནི་མི་གཙང་བ་དང་། བདེ་བ་དང་། རྟག་པ་དང་བདག་ཏུ་འཛིན་པའོ། །མི་གཙང་བ་ལ་གཙང་བར་ཕྱིན་ཅི་ལོག་ཏུ་འཛིན་པ་སྤོང་བའི་ཕྱིར་ལུས་དྲན་པ་ཉེ་བར་གཞག་པ་བསྒོམས་ཏེ། ལུས་ལ་ནི་གཙོ་བོར་མི་གཙང་བའི་མཚན་ཉིད་དུ་བསྒོམ་པར་བཅོམ་ལྡན་འདས་ཀྱིས་གསུངས་སོ། །སྡུག་བསྔལ་ལ་བདེ་བར་འཛིན་པའི་ཕྱིན་ཅི་ལོག་ཏུ་འཛིན་པ་སྤང་བའི་ཕྱིར་ཚོར་བ་དྲན་པ་ཉེ་བར་གཞག་པ་བསྒོམས་ཏེ། ཇི་སྲིད་དུ་ཚོར་བ་ཐམས་ཅད་ཀྱང་སྡུག་བསྔལ་རྣམ་པ་གསུམ་དང་འབྲེལ་ཏོ་ཞེས། བཅོམ་ལྡན་འདས་ཀྱིས་གསུངས་པའི་ཕྱིར་རོ། །མི་རྟག་པ་ལ་རྟག་པར་ཕྱིན་ཅི་ལོག་ཏུ་འཛིན་པའི་གཉེན་པོར། སེམས་དྲན་པ་ཉེ་བར་གཞག་པ་བསྒོམས་ཏེ། སེམས་འདི་ཡང་སྐད་ཅིག་མ་རེ་རེ་ལ་འདོད་ཆགས་དང་བཅས་པ་

དང་། འདོད་ཆགས་མེད་པ་ལ་སོགས་པ་རྣམ་པ་གཞན་དང་གཞན་
དུ་འགྱུར་བའི་ཕྱིར་རོ། །བདག་མེད་པ་ལ་བདག་ཏུ་འཛིན་པའི་ཕྱིན་
ཅི་ལོག་སྤོང་བའི་ཕྱིར། ཆོས་དྲན་པ་ཉེ་བར་གཞག་པ་བསྒོམས་ཏེ།
འདོད་ཆགས་ལ་སོགས་པས་ནི་ཀུན་ནས་ཉོན་མོངས་པར་འགྱུར།
དད་པ་ལ་སོགས་པས་ནི་རྣམ་པར་བྱང་བར་འགྱུར་བར་ཟད་ཀྱི། འདི་
ནི་ཀུན་ནས་ཉོན་མོངས་པར་བྱེད་པ་དང་། རྣམ་པར་བྱང་བར་བྱེད་པའི་
བྱེད་པ་པོ་དང་། བདག་མེད་པ་ཁོང་དུ་ཆུད་ན། བདག་ཏུ་འཛིན་པའི་
ཕྱིན་ཅི་ལོག་དང་བྲལ་བར་འགྱུར་རོ། །བདེན་པ་བཞི་ལ་འཇུག་པ་ནི་
ལུས་དྲན་པ་ཉེ་བར་གཞག་པ་བསྒོམས་པས། སྡུག་བསྔལ་གྱི་བདེན་
པ་ལ་འཇུག་སྟེ། ལུས་ཀྱི་རང་བཞིན་མཐོང་ན་སྐྱེ་རྒ་ན་འཆི་ལ་སོགས་
པའི་སྡུག་བསྔལ་རྣམ་པ་སྣ་ཚོགས་དང་ལྡན་པར་རྟོགས་པར་འགྱུར་
བའི་ཕྱིར་རོ། །ཚོར་བ་དྲན་པ་ཉེ་བར་གཞག་པ་བསྒོམས་པས་ཀུན་
འབྱུང་གི་བདེན་པ་ལ་འཇུག་སྟེ། ཚོར་བ་བདེ་བ་ལ་བརྟེན་ནས་ནི་སྲེད་
པ་སྐྱེ། ཚོར་བ་སྡུག་བསྔལ་བའི་རྒྱུས་ནི་ཞེ་སྡང་སྐྱེ་ལ། ཚོར་བ་བདེ་
བ་ཡང་མ་ཡིན་སྡུག་བསྔལ་ཡང་མ་ཡིན་པའི་རྒྱུས་ནི་གཏི་མུག་སྐྱེ།
འདོད་ཆགས་དང་། ཞེ་སྡང་དང་། གཏི་མུག་གི་རྒྱུས་ཚེ་རབས་གཞན་
གྱི་ཕུང་པོ་འབྱུང་བར་འགྱུར་རོ་ཞེས་རྟོགས་པའི་ཕྱིར་རོ། །སེམས་དྲན་
པ་ཉེ་བར་གཞག་པ་བསྒོམས་པས་ནི་འགོག་པའི་བདེན་པ་ལ་འཇུག་
སྟེ། སེམས་སྐད་ཅིག་མ་རེ་རེ་ལ་འཇིག་པའི་རང་བཞིན་བདག་མེད་
པའི་མཚན་ཉིད་དུ་མཐོང་ན་མྱ་ངན་ལས་འདས་པ་ལས་བདག་ཆད་
པར་འགྱུར་རོ། ཞེས་འཇིག་པ་མི་འབྱུང་བའི་ཕྱིར་རོ། །ཆོས་དྲན་པ་
ཉེ་བར་གཞག་པ་བསྒོམས་པས་ལམ་གྱི་བདེན་པ་ལ་འཇུག་སྟེ། ཀུན་
ནས་ཉོན་མོངས་པ་དང་། རྣམ་པར་བྱང་བའི་ཕྱོགས་གཉིས་མཐོང་

ནས་ཀུན་ནས་ཉོན་མོངས་པ་སྤྱོང་བའི་ཕྱིར། རྣམ་པར་བྱང་བའི་ཆོས་ལ་རྟེན་པར་བྱེད་པས་སོ། །བྲལ་བ་ནི་ལུས་ལ་སོགས་པ་བསྒོམས་པས། གནས་ངན་ལེན་པ་ཐམས་ཅད་དང་བྲལ་བར་འགྱུར་བའི་ཕྱིར་རོ།

།རྣམ་གྲངས་གཞན་དུ་ན་འཇིག་རྟེན་པ་དག་ནི་ཕལ་ཆེར་ཕུང་པོ་ལྔ་ལ་ཕུང་པོ་ཙམ་མམ་ཆོས་ཙམ་དུ་ཡང་དག་པ་ཇི་ལྟ་བ་བཞིན་དུ་ཁོང་དུ་མ་ཆུད་པས་འདི་ལྟ་སྟེ། བདག་དེ་ལུས་ལ་གནས་ཤིང་ཚོར་བ་བདེ་བ་དང་སྡུག་བསྔལ་བ་ཀུན་ནས་ཉོན་མོངས་པར་བྱེད་པ་དང་། ཆོས་དང་ཆོས་མ་ཡིན་པས་རྣམ་པར་བྱང་བ་དང་། །ཀུན་ནས་ཉོན་མོངས་པར་འགྱུར་རོ་ཞེས་འཛིན་པ་བཟློག་པའི་ཕྱིར། དྲན་པ་ཉེ་བར་གཞག་པ་བཞི་གསུངས་ཏེ། དེ་ལ་ལུས་ནི་བདག་གི་རྟེན་གྱི་དངོས་པོའོ་ཞེས་རྨོངས་པ་བསལ་བའི་ཕྱིར་ལུས་དྲན་པ་ཉེ་བར་གཞག་པ་བསྟན་ཏེ། ལུས་འདི་མི་གཙང་བ་དང་སྡུག་བསྔལ་གྱི་གནས་ཀྱི་དངོས་པོ་ཡིན་གྱི། བདག་གི་དངོས་པོ་ནི་མ་ཡིན་ཞེས་བྱ་བའི་དོན་ཏོ། །ཚོར་བ་ནི་བདག་དེས་ཀུན་ཏུ་སྤྱོད་པར་བྱ་བའི་དངོས་པོ་ཡིན་ནོ་ཞེས་རྨོངས་པ་བསལ་བའི་ཕྱིར་རོ། །ཚོར་བ་དྲན་པ་ཉེ་བར་གཞག་པ་བཤད་དེ། །ཚོར་བ་ཐམས་ཅད་ནི་སྡུག་བསྔལ་བ་ཡིན་གྱིས། བདག་དེས་ཀུན་ཏུ་སྤྱོད་པར་བྱ་བ་ནི་མ་ཡིན་ཞེས་བྱ་བའི་དོན་ཏོ། །སེམས་དང་ཡིད་དང་རྣམ་པར་ཤེས་པ་ལ་བདག་གི་དངོས་པོར་འཛིན་པ་བསལ་བའི་ཕྱིར། སེམས་དྲན་པ་ཉེ་བར་གཞག་པ་བསྒོམ་པ་བསྟན་ཏེ། སེམས་ནི་སྐད་ཅིག་མའི་རང་བཞིན་ཡིན་གྱི། བདག་གི་རང་བཞིན་ནི་མ་ཡིན་ནོ་ཞེས་བྱ་བའི་དོན་ཏོ། །ཆོས་ཀྱིས་ནི་བདག་དེ་ཉིད་ཀུན་ནས་ཉོན་མོངས་པ་དང་། རྣམ་པར་བྱང་བར་བྱེད་དོ་ཞེས་རྨོངས་པའི་ཕྱིར་

ཆོས་དྲན་པ་ཉེ་བར་གཞག་པ་བསྒོམ་པ་བཤད་དེ། འདོད་ཆགས་ལ་
སོགས་པས་ཀུན་ནས་ཉོན་མོངས་པར་བྱེད་ཅིང་། དད་པ་ལ་སོགས་
པས་སེམས་རྣམ་པར་བྱང་བར་བྱེད་པར་ཟད་ཀྱི། བདག་མེད་པའི་
རང་བཞིན་ཡིན་པས། དེ་ལ་ནི་ཀུན་ནས་ཉོན་མོངས་པ་དང་། རྣམ་
པར་བྱང་བར་འགྱུར་བ་མི་སྲིད་དོ་ཞེས་བྱ་བའི་ཐ་ཚིག་གོ། ...

About the Author

Shamar Rinpoche (1952–2014), also known as Mipham Chökyi Lodrö, was the Fourteenth Shamarpa. The Shamarpa, or "Red Hat Lama of Tibet," represents Tibetan Buddhism's second oldest reincarnate lineage after the Karmapa's lineage. Born in Derge, East Tibet, Shamar Rinpoche was recognized by the Sixteenth Gyalwa Karmapa in 1957 and enthroned as the Fourteenth Shamarpa in 1963. After years of study with Buddhist scholars, he began spreading the Buddha Dharma in 1980, teaching at Karma Kagyu centers worldwide. Shamar Rinpoche was a highly accomplished Buddhist master and teacher, esteemed and valued by numerous students of Buddhism globally. In 1996, he initiated the establishment of Bodhi Path Buddhist Centers, a network spanning multiple continents, advocating a non-sectarian approach to meditation. Furthermore, he founded several non-profit organizations over the years and actively participated in charitable endeavors, including projects to provide education for impoverished children and initiatives dedicated to promoting animal rights.

About the translator

Dr. Martina Draszczyk holds a PhD in Buddhist Studies and Tibetology. Since the early 1980s, she has learned and practiced under the guidance of Shamar Rinpoche, repeatedly interpreting for him since the late 1980s. From 1992 to 2005, she served as an interpreter at the Karmapa International Buddhist Institute (KIBI) in New Delhi while concurrently pursuing her own studies there. She completed her doctoral thesis at the Department for South Asian, Tibetan, and Buddhist Studies at the University of Vienna, where she also worked as a lecturer and researcher. Additionally, she has served as a guest professor at the University of Vienna and McGill University in Montréal, Canada. She has authored several translations and books on Buddhist views and meditation, and she teaches at Buddhist centers in Europe.

Publishing finished
in January 2025 by Pulsio
Publisher Number: 4030
Legal Deposit: January 2025
Printed in Bulgaria